CELINE UWINEZA

Untamed

BEYOND FREEDOM

GW00585202

A transformational healing journey,
after surviving the 1994 Genocide

First published by Celine Uwineza, 2019
Copyright © 2019 by Celine Uwineza

ISBN 978-10919-7-508-8

Edited by Gael Tunga Rutembesa and Phillipa Mitchell
Cover design and typesetting by Gregg Davies
(www.greggdavies.com)
Creative direction by Inkstain and Envision Rwanda

To my maternal grandparents, Ruvuzumutego Leonidas and
Joyce Kankindi stoned to death.

To my paternal grandfather, Eustache Kajuga
shot to death by multiple bullets.

To my Uncle Huss Mugwaneza and his wife Annie Mugwaneza,
shot dead in their home.

To my mother, Norah Mukeshimana, my sister Kayitesi Claudette,
my sister Francine Ingabire, and my brother Claude Murengezi,
hacked and burned to death.

To my family whose bodies were never found:

My Uncle Maharangari, his wife Flora, and their five children—
Gilbert, Norbert, Mugeni, Liliose, and Clarisse—shot dead one after
the other.

My Aunt Françoise, her husband Kayumba and their three children
—Lise, Dimitri, and Manzi— pursued and killed in the hills as
they ran for their lives.

My Aunt Antoinette Kamisheke, her husband Kurujyishuri Joel, and
their seven children, Victoire-Aimee Umuhoza, Clementine
Girumuhoza, Felix Ntitetereza, Ferdinand Mwizerwa, Christine
Uwase, Clement Ndayishimiye and Yvette Uwizeye, whose last
moments remain unknown.

To the one million souls—especially each of the children killed during
the 1994 Genocide against the Tutsi—
This memoir is dedicated to you. I honor your lives cut short. Your
lives matters. Your memories are alive now and forever more.

Foreword

Sunk in existential suffering and utter unworthiness, the human quest for meaning and significance is unending.

As a little girl, Celine Uwineza had to face the unspeakable worst. As a young woman, her life story merged with that of a great angelic soul, Anne Heyman-Merrin of blessed memory. Anne established a model youth village for orphans from the Genocide Against the Tutsi in Rwanda, based on the Jewish People's experience of tragedy - and renewal. It is at Agahozo-Shalom Youth Village where Celine opened her heart, and truly dedicated herself to healing the suffering of others, that the Lord restored her trust in mankind.

Celine exemplifies the restoration of the human spirit from brokenness to wholeness. Her life, marked by transformational healing, also echoes the greater healing process of her motherland, Rwanda, emanating a message that the world today must hear. Through her story, we are reassured that the mending of a broken human heart - Tikkun HaLev in Hebrew - is not only achievable, but is in fact the core of one's divine life mission.

"Lord, when I consider your heavens, the work of your fingers, the moon and the stars, which You have ordained, what is man that You are mindful of him? For You have made him a little lower than the angels, and You have crowned him with glory and honor". Psalm 8

Dr. Chaim Peri

Founder, The Village Way Institute

Yemin Orde, Mt. Carmel, Israel

Introduction

"There is no greater agony than bearing an untold story inside you."
Maya Angelou.

During the Genocide against the Tutsi in Rwanda in 1994, we were hunted to death. By the time it was over, my mother, my three siblings, my grandparents and more than thirty other members of my extended family had been brutally murdered. At ten years old, I became a refugee in my own country, walking and running for miles on end amidst crowds of terrified, unfamiliar faces.

I grew up battling anger and desperation, grappling with questions I could not answer. The killers were our neighbors, classmates, and colleagues. They were nephews, sons, daughters, and grandchildren. I had so many questions: Were they born killers? If not, how were they taught to kill in such a short time? Why had evil and hatred triumphed to such an extent? Why did my family have to die? Why had I survived? I was not the only one fighting this battle—all Rwandans were striving to rebuild themselves and our country.

One day, the inner battle that had been boiling inside me erupted. I would be woken by recurring nightmares of my grandparents being stoned to death, visions of my family being brutally murdered flashing through my mind. The time had come for me to face my traumatic past head on, and allow my ten-year-old self to grieve and be set free. I realized that Rwanda's transformation had to begin with me, so I resolved to play my part in this quest for a bright future. I embarked upon a journey of healing to deal with the trauma that was preventing me from soaring to my full potential and living a full life. Through expert help, I committed to moving from a satisfactory existence to one of excellence, using my God-given talents.

Our stories matter. They have the potential to inspire others to share their stories, and impact their communities in return. I chose to write this book to heal from my wounds, to give a voice to my family, to defy the Genocide denials, and to highlight the importance of memory preservation as a tool to fight against Genocide ideology and violence. The book is also an opportunity to recognize Rwandans' journey of healing, resilience, and courage. Most of all, I wrote this book so that I would never forget *my* story. I hope that it will reach and inspire many to share their own stories of courage, and that it will be counted among other Rwandan and African transformational stories.

My vision is to see the youth of today and tomorrow equipped with the skills to take a stand against violence, with zero tolerance to discrimination, poverty, and mediocrity. My prayer is to see them positively impact Africa and the world.

My name is Celine Uwineza—an African child, a Rwandan daughter born and raised in the land of a thousand dreams, stories, and hills.

"Trauma generates emotions, and unless we process these emotions at the time the trauma occurs, they become stuck in our mind and body. Instead of healing from the wounding event, the trauma stays in our body as energy in our unconscious, affecting our life until we uncover it and process it out. The healthy flow and processing of distressing emotions, such as anger, sadness, shame, and fear, is essential to healing from childhood trauma as an adult." **Psychology Today. (**Steps to Healing Childhood Trauma as an Adult_ Andrea Brandt, Ph.D)

Part I

1

A Letter To My Mother

October 25, 2015

*D*ear Mama,

    My counselor asked me to write to you. I am not sure I under-stand why, and I don't know where to start.

Too much has happened since we last saw each other. It has been twenty-two years, but it feels like yesterday. My ten-year-old self is still waiting for you to come back and take her with you, but I think that where you went was a one-way ticket, and my time to join you hasn't yet come.

I hope you can still hear me from where you are in Heaven. I have so much to share, so sit tight, Mum. I have been waiting and longing for the day when I'll tell you every single detail of what happened after you were all killed. Could you tell my sisters, Kayitesi and Francine, and my brother Claude that I will write to them too?

I stopped for a moment and looked around me. I was sitting in a room at Ndera Neuropsychiatric Hospital, having just been diagnosed with Post Traumatic Stress Disorder and depression. It was my third therapy session. My therapist had proposed that I write to my mother and my siblings who lost their lives during the 1994 Genocide against the Tutsi. She said that by revisiting the memories, I would give the ten-year-old me a platform to grieve, regain my strength, and move forward to meet the thirty-three-year-old me.

Although my therapist emphasized focusing on the areas of success in my life and my hopes for the future, I struggled to relate to them. Too many questions filled my head. What is the meaning of life? What is success? Why is there life, and then sudden death? Why am I feeling this way? Why this sudden blockage?

I was not tired, but all I wanted to do was withdraw and stay in my bed. How I longed for a button that I could click where I would return to being the playful, joyful, and lively Celine that I once was.

Why can't I just go back to normal?

There was soft music playing in the room. I looked outside, lost in my thoughts, feeling empty and alone. It was then that something occurred to me that I had not considered during my other sessions: While before all I had been able to do was cry and sit quietly, this time I noticed the other patients around me. Some were suffering from mental illness; a young girl was walking around in circles like a zombie; a man was seated on the ground talking to himself. I watched other groups of people sitting together, deep in discussion and, in that moment, I asked myself how in the world I had ended up there. I had survived the Genocide together with my father and my brother, Johnny. I had two new siblings, Lyrette and Michael, who brought so much joy to my soul. I had an incredible extended family. I was married to a wonderful man. I had good friends. I had a brilliant career as the director of human resources at Agahozo-Shalom Youth Village. I was coherent, and I had most certainly not lost my mind.

Being a born again Christian, I came to the conclusion that I was simply being ungrateful. After all, what more could I wish for in life? There were so many people suffering in the world and here I was, completely blessed, yet complaining about feeling lost and overshadowed by sadness, and unable to celebrate the magnificent abundance in my life. I stared blankly ahead at the window, tears sliding hopelessly down my cheeks.

"Celine?" I heard the gentle voice of my therapist calling my name.

"Yes?" I responded, wiping the tears from my eyes.

"Do you want to share what is making you cry?" she asked.

I exhaled deeply and remained silent for a few seconds, gathering my jumbled thoughts.

My therapist, a nun who had recently completed her specialization in Trauma and Post Traumatic Stress Disorder in the USA, nodded and looked at me sympathetically as I explained my predicament. Naturally empathetic, she had an interesting way of doing therapy, and I loved her playful spirit—things were far too complicated in my head for me to have a rigid therapist. I watched her jotting down a few lines in her notebook before suddenly looking at me.

"Celine, can we try something?" she asked, "I want to give you an exercise to do at home."

I nodded, and she continued, "When you get home today—or even tomorrow or over the next few days, take a moment and try to recall the last time you felt happiness and joy in your life. When you remember, write it down. You can tell me about it in our session next week, and we will discuss it in detail."

"Can you do that for me?" she asked gently.

It was a strange request, but after a brief moment of hesitation, I agreed to do it.

She accompanied me to the hospital's waiting area where my aunt, Mama Lily, was sitting. Mama Lily took my hand, and we walked along the pavement to the parking lot. She was one of two of my Mum's sisters. A professional nurse who understood psychological needs better than me, Mama Lily had been driving me to my therapy sessions since day one. Gilbert, my husband, would wait at home for me, a warm lunch prepared for when I returned.

I never spoke about my therapy, but I always reassured them that it was helpful, even though it was still unclear to me whether it was helping me or not.

While driving home from Ndera to Kanombe, I pulled my chair back and lay down. Mama Lily looked at me worriedly. "This must be heavy for you. How are you feeling, dearest?"

I looked up at her. "The back of my head is so heavy. I feel tired and cannot wait to go to bed."

"I can imagine," she empathized. "Take a nap after lunch. I hope you will feel better."

Recalling Memories

*T*he following day, I took a notebook and a pen, sat down at my favorite spot in the living room, and began to write. My husband had gone to work, and I was on sick leave, so I was alone in the house.

While casting my mind back to when I last experienced joy in my life, I felt a smile creeping in. It was July 1993 when my parents, my three siblings, and I took our last trip to visit my maternal grandparents. These vacations were long-awaited by everyone in my family. Being town folk, experiencing life in the countryside fascinated us. We had cousins of the same age, and my parents, uncles, and aunties made a point of ensuring that all the children met at our grandparents' and spent at least one month together during our vacations. It was on my grandparents' farm that we first saw a cow giving birth, how the mother and calf were taken care of, and how they grazed. It was there that we ran and played in the fields while Grandpa showed the grown-ups his agricultural projects and the different types of bananas he was growing.

There was no way that I could have known that 1993 would be the last year that I would enjoy these treasured moments.

We bundled into Mum's car, a double cabin, with our luggage packed in the back. Dad was driving, with Mum in the passenger seat. Mum was a beautiful, God-fearing woman who sang in the church choir. Just like my grandparents, she taught us God's word and how to pray. Her values reflected the godly principles she instilled in us. I remember her as a caring person who loved her husband, her family, her colleagues, and her friends deeply. She was endlessly patient, despite her strict nature.

As soon as we had hit the open road Mum reached forward and pressed play on the only tape that she ever listened to—*Abasaruzi*, an Adventist choir that she loved dearly. My brother Claude immediately protested as the car filled with the familiar lyrics and melodies. "But Mum, you have been playing these songs non-stop for two years. We know them all by heart, and frankly, we are tired of them. Can we please play something different?" With MC Hammer, Ace of Base and Koffi Olomide dominating the airwaves back then, I was certain that he would have rather been listening to them instead of *Abasaruzi*.

Claude was usually not one to express his feelings so openly. Even at twenty years of age, he was a shy young man with a smile and laugh that created an aura of serenity around him. He was handsome, and always clean, neat, and smartly dressed—it is no wonder that he was so popular with the high school girls. He was an aspiring journalist who enjoyed listening to the news, reading newspapers, and reporting his findings to us.

My sisters, Kayitesi and Francine, laughed at Claude's protests. "Mum," he implored, "The tape itself is tired. Give it a break."

Francine, thirteen years old at the time, was the closest sibling I had in terms of age. She was the one with whom I had daily conversations and played with most of the time. Being more responsible, she was always put in charge of children's playtime at home. To add to her cheerful nature, she demonstrated her wisdom through her obedience, always weighing her decisions carefully to avoid getting into trouble with Mum and Dad.

Kayitesi was a bright nineteen-year-old woman. Because of her self-motivated hard work and outstanding marks in school, Dad believed that nothing in the world would ever be difficult for her and that she would grow up to be a medical doctor. She was *that* child who never gave her parents a hard time. She was so much like Mum—strict, with the same strength of character. She was a leader—my role model—and I wanted to be just like her. Her hair was always well-combed, her nails immaculately manicured, and she was always clean and neat. One thing she couldn't do, however, was cook—not even an omelet.

"Itunda mwabujijwe n'Imana niryo mwariye....lalalala." [1]Kayitesi sang, making it clear how well everyone had memorized the song that Mum had tortured our ears with for so long.

I didn't care about the music—I was impatient to see my cousins and spend the entire month with them.

"We are going on a road trip that will last many hours," Mum finally said, never one to give in. "We need God's protection, and these songs allow the Holy Spirit to fill the air—don't you think?"

"In fact," she added, "we didn't pray prior to leaving the house." She turned to Dad and asked him if he would pull aside and pray for us and every other traveler who was taking the same journey to our grandparents.

My maternal grandparents lived in Butare, in the Gikonko sector in the southern province of Rwanda. We all loved them very much, and they loved and cherished us in return. Grandpa would allow us to take turns braiding his soft, gray hair. I remember how he laughed as he watched us behave like professional hair stylists, even though we were unable to keep his cornrows.

Grandma always had a hard time keeping us in order, especially during church services where ten of us would be seated in the same row, fidgeting and playing with our chairs.

They both loved God. Grandpa immersed himself in his Bible—the only book he read—and planted the seed of love in our hearts. "My children," he would say, "Love is what will take you to Heaven, and you don't want to miss Heaven, do you? Love each other and love everyone around you so that you can get to Heaven one day."

Grandma taught us God's word and Christian values. She also taught us to love and be at peace with everyone, using the scriptures for emphasis: "My children," she would say, quoting *Romans 12: 19-21*, "Never revenge. Learn how to live at peace with everyone. Revenge is God's."

She told us a story of how, in 1959, Grandpa's brothers were beaten and killed for being Tutsis. Despite that, he still lived in the same community as the perpetrators, and we played with their grandchildren who would come and ask for milk and bananas—which we would duly give to them. "That verse is the one that kept your grandpa at peace," she said.

As the beautiful memories continued replaying in my mind, my heart froze as I recalled how after the Genocide, my Mum's sister, Helene Sebuharara (Mama Lily), returned to our grandparents' home to see if they had survived. Everyone's hopes were high that, because they were in their golden years, nobody would see the need to take their lives. Alas, they were not spared. Instead, they were thrown into an empty pit and stoned to death. To add to our loss, my paternal Uncle Maharangari, his wife and their five children, my cousins, were shot dead in Kigali.

---

1. "The God' forbidden fruit is what you ate"

Part II

3

The Genocide

*D*ay one of the therapy exercise left me emotionally weak. I was reluctant to continue, and I told my therapist that recalling the memories was causing more damage, but she encouraged me to keep writing down my memories as they came to mind. Over time, I discovered that the process of recollection began to still my mind, unlocking my soul so that I could listen to my inner self.

Early 1994

It was the week of Easter and, like many other ten-year-olds, my heart was filled with hope and excitement as we prepared to celebrate this seasonal holiday. Easter was synonymous with family gatherings and fun-filled parties complete with food and countless games played with my cousins and friends. We would wear the new clothes that we had been given for Easter. I would spend the week daydreaming about the church service that Sunday, where I would play a special role as one of the women who cried over Jesus' cross in the Easter Sunday play. I had been performing in these plays since I was three years old, thanks to Mum.

At 5:00 p.m. on the evening of the 6th of April 1994, I heard Mum calling me.

"Celine! Celine! Where are you?"

I was always on the move, playing in the garden, or mischievously planning pranks to annoy Francine. She was so easygoing, and I would laugh when she discovered my intentions and looked at me like the crazy little sister I was. Mum called again. She hated it when we didn't respond immediately, or if we took our time to get to her.

"Go and wash your hands and wear a warm pullover," she told me, "We're going to visit Uncle Huss."

"Let's go and see if we can gather information from Uncle Huss about Dad and Grandma," she said to my siblings, who were watching television in the living room, "We need to know if they crossed the border and made it safely to Goma." My father and his mother, my grandmother, were en route to Kinshasa to attend the burial of Dad's brother-in-law who had died on the fourth of April. The family had decided to send them to represent the family in the Democratic Republic of the Congo (DRC), formerly Zaire. They had left early on the morning of the sixth of April, traveling by road, their plan was to pass through the border at Goma and into the DRC. Uncle Huss would have received word if they had arrived there safely.

Visiting Uncle Huss's house was a real treat. Uncle Huss' wife, Annie, was a white Belgian native. They had the largest garden I had ever seen, and I loved running and playing in it. "We're leaving in thirty minutes," Mum shouted out as we readied ourselves. The house was bustling with excitement. At the time, I was more interested in Aunty Annie's food and the chocolate dessert which usually followed, than whether my father and grandmother had reached the DRC.

At 6:00 p.m. Claude drove us to Uncle Huss', which was ten minutes away. Mum was seated in the passenger seat, with my sisters and I in the back. We spotted Françoise, my former nanny, along the road. Mum had employed Françoise as a cashier in her shop.

"Mum!" I shouted. "Look! Look, there's Françoise."

Claude slowed down and stopped the car. "Is everything okay, Françoise?" Mum asked, "You are visiting very late." Françoise greeted us, explaining that she had just left the store that she and Mum managed, and was going to spend the night with us instead of returning to her studio apartment in Nyamirambo sector, close to where the shop was located. "I miss the children," she said.

"Ok. We'll be back in an hour or two," Mum told her.

Claude started up the engine again, and we continued along the road to Uncle Huss' where we found Aunty Annie, their son Kiko, my paternal grandfather, and another cousin, Felix, waiting for us. Grandpa was a pastor, and whenever he greeted us with one of his warm hugs, he would ask us to recite Psalm 23. The trick was to run from him immediately after the hug to avoid being asked to recite it.

As soon as we pulled up into the driveway, I jumped out of the car and ran to the garden, only to hear Mum calling, "Celine! Celine! Where are you? Don't you try and run outside. It's getting dark." I was disappointed. What was I going to do if I couldn't run and play?

The television was on inside the house, and the family was discussing which news program to watch. With little interest in the news, I headed to the kitchen where Ancila, the cook, gave me a piece of cake and invited me to watch her prepare the evening's refreshments.

My uncle arrived home and popped his head through the kitchen door. He hugged me, and then joined the grown-ups in the living room. It must have been about an hour later that I heard Mum calling us for prayer—led by our paternal grandpa—and then we got back in the car and drove home. As we drove away, I longed to return to the big garden and run and play with my cousins. But this would be the last time I would see them. Uncle Huss, his wife Annie, my paternal grandfather, my cousin Felix, and Ancila were all killed on April 7, 1994.

4

The Beginning Of The End

*I*t was 7:30 p.m. when we arrived home. I found Françoise in the kitchen. She was serving food, and I stayed close by her side during dinner. After we had eaten, I was told to brush my teeth and go to sleep. So I said goodnight to everyone, hugged Mum, and went to bed, looking forward to the next day. Knowing there was no school, I anticipated nothing but more fun and games.

At 6:00 a.m. on the 7th of April, I was woken by alarmingly loud noises outside. I thought I was dreaming and tried to go back to sleep, but the noises continued. I was frightened. It sounded like gunshots and grenades, similar to what we would hear in the movies. Francine, with whom I shared the bedroom, was also awake. Confused and seeking comfort, I asked her, "What are those noises? What's happening? "Don't worry," said Francine reassuringly, "It's probably policemen in pursuit of the bad guys. Once they catch them, it will stop."

I got out of my bed and climbed into hers. We huddled together, waiting for it all to end.

For more than an hour, it sounded as if the war was happening right outside the window, in our yard. Francine and I were too afraid to leave our bedroom, but we eventually decided to ask Claude, who was always well-informed and up to date with the latest news, if he knew why the policemen were shooting.

We entered the living room to a strange sight. Mum was sitting on the sofa with a hopeless look on her face. Claude was staring strangely at the radio. My other sister, Kayitesi, was nudging him.

What's happening, Claude?" she asked, "Why are there gunshots?"

"President Habyarimana is dead," said Claude, "His plane was shot down."

"What does that mean?" Kayitesi stammered, "It is a good thing, right? He was a very bad man."

Mum rose slowly from her chair. When she spoke, her voice was filled with sadness and fear. "My children," she said, slowly and deliberately, "This is very bad news. It's the end of us all."

We watched as she disappeared from the living room and into her bedroom, closing the door behind her.

I didn't understand the conversation, but it seemed like something was supposed to happen following the news . Many questions were running through my head. The President is dead? His plane was shot down? He was a bad man? What does this have to do with us? And what did Mum mean by saying it was the end of us all?

I was also hungry.

"When are we having breakfast?" I asked. Everyone looked at me strangely. Francine took me to the kitchen. Françoise was there, and she had already prepared breakfast. I was relieved that there was somebody in the house who wasn't acting weird.

As I helped Françoise to set the table, the slow, disturbing classical music playing on the radio caught my attention. I asked Claude why the radio was playing the same song over and over again. He looked at me as if he didn't hear what I had asked, and said, "Let's have breakfast. Go and get Mum and bring her in."

My stomach rumbling, I went and knocked at Mum's door. When I opened it, I found her standing in the middle of the room, staring blankly into space. I had never seen her like that before and didn't know what to make of it. "Come and have breakfast, Mum," I said. She turned and looked at me as if I was speaking in a foreign language.

"Huh?"

I repeated, "Come for breakfast. I am hungry."

She came towards me and grabbed my arm, pulling me as we walked down the corridor in silence towards the dining room. She would usually do this when she was about to punish me. I wondered what I had done wrong, other than standing in the doorway and calling her for breakfast. We found everyone seated at the dining table. Nobody said a word. The gunshots and bombs from outside and the strange music from the radio was growing louder and clearer. Nobody paid attention to the omelets on the table.

"What is wrong with everyone?" I wondered. I remembered what Francine had told me earlier that morning, and repeated her words out loud: "Don't worry. It's probably policemen in pursuit of the bad guys. Once they catch them, it will stop."

Everybody looked at me empathetically, but the room remained silent.

"Mum, can we pray?" I asked.

We ate breakfast. The omelet was good, but the mood around the table was gloomy. Mum stood up to make a phone call. I could hear her trying to reach Uncle Huss, without success. *"Ntibikunda Maman Lily nawe byanze "* she said ("It's not going through. Mama Lily's phone is dead too").

She looked so lost and hopeless. She was restless, pacing back and forth across the room. I could not see the seriousness of the situation. I wondered why she didn't think to call back later, or for us to drive to uncle Huss' if she wanted to talk to him so desperately.

The voice on the radio continued to repeat the same announcement every five minutes: '*Nta muntu wemerewe gusohoka hanze. Abanyarwanda mwese musabwe kuguna mungo zanyu!*" (All Rwandans are required to stay indoors. Nobody is allowed to go out."

I did not realize that the message applied to us.

I returned to my room after breakfast, grabbed my copy of *The Adventures of Tintin* and read it before taking a shower and heading outside to play as I did on any other holiday. The gunshots were still rampant, but they did not bother me. "Let me go outside the gate," I thought to myself, "Maybe I will see where the bad guys are hiding and inform the police, and they will stop firing."

I needed Mum to stop behaving so strangely, and for my life to return to normal.

I walked outside. I opened the small gate to our compound. The road outside was deserted. There were no bad guys, no policemen, no dogs, no cars. There was nothing. I wondered where the noises were coming from and where the policemen that were firing the guns were.

Mum suddenly appeared beside me. She tightly grabbed my hand and dragged me towards the house.

"Mum!" I wailed, "You are hurting me!" But she wouldn't listen. She was hell-bent on getting me back indoors. We reached the living room where everyone was staring at me with fear in their eyes. "Celine, you are not allowed to go outside," Mum snapped at me, "Stay indoors and stay away from the windows. Do you understand?"

I looked at her, frightened, as she repeated her words more sternly, "Do you understand?"

I nodded.

"Watch her," she told Kayitesi, "Don't let her out of your sight."

I felt the fear slowly rising inside me.

Kayitesi took me aside. "Celine, this is not a game. There are no policemen, and there are no bad guys. This is a real war, and it's very serious. It's important that we listen to Mum and do what she says. Okay?"

I nodded. My heart was thumping in my throat. Kayitesi told me to go to her bedroom and read. As I walked down the passage, I wondered what war was. Everything had changed in an instant. One moment, I was being told that everything would be okay once the policemen caught the bad guys, and the next I was told something completely different—and terrifying.

Unable to stay in the room alone, I returned to the living room where Kayitesi told me to sit on the sofa and remain quiet. Mum spoke to somebody on the phone, and a neighbor's house worker came to ask for food. Mum gave him rice, potatoes, and beans. Claude was still listening to the radio. Kayitesi stayed at Mum's side. They spoke in low voices. Francine was seated quietly. I could tell that she was frightened.

5

The Prayer

$\mathcal{A}$ t 1:00 p.m. we gathered for lunch. Mum looked more serious than ever. It was clear that she had something important to tell us, and that she wanted our full, undivided attention. In a low, stern tone, she began to speak.

"Things are going badly, my children. People are dying. Tutsis are being killed, and we might die as well. But don't worry. Our Heavenly Father will welcome us, and we will all be reunited in heaven."

We all stared at her, wide-eyed with fear.

"I want you to repeat this prayer," she continued, "I want you to memorize every piece of it and believe it, and when the Interahamwe come, repeat it in your heart. Make sure you don't forget any word of it."

None of what Mum said made sense in my head. What is the meaning of dying? How do people die? Why can't we just continue our normal and beautiful life? I love it the way it is. I don't want to go anywhere.

Mum began to pray, "*Data wa twese, mwami mana, utubabarire ibicumuro byacu, ubabarire ababitugirira, utweze kandi utwakire mu bwami buhoraho. Mw'Izina rya Yesu Kristu.* Amen." (Our heavenly Father, Our God, forgive all our sins, forgive those who sin against us, cleanse us Lord and welcome us in eternal life, in Jesus name. Amen.)

"Go ahead and repeat the prayer," she said.

I wondered what kind of prayer this was, and why nobody mentioned anything about the food we were about to eat for lunch. Claude was a bit annoyed, but Mum was firm, determined that we memorize it. I knew that if we did not follow her instructions, we would never have eaten that lunch.

We repeated the prayer five times. By the third time, we weren't taking Mum seriously, but she made us repeat it a fourth time and, by the fifth, it was crystal clear to everyone that she meant business. After memorizing the prayer, we ate, and I was sent for the afternoon nap that I hated so much. It didn't take me long to fall asleep, though.

The sensation of something hard and cold pressing against my arm woke me. It was 4:00 p.m. As I opened my eyes, the chilling figure of a tall, dark-skinned soldier loomed over me. He shoved me with his gun, angrily telling me to wake up—and quickly. I looked around hoping to see a familiar face, but there was nobody. I was overcome with terror.

"Go, find your family," he growled at me.

I hurriedly got out of bed and walked ahead of him as he shoved me towards the living room. My whole family was there, seated quietly. They were frozen with fear. Another soldier stood in the room with them. He was lean, with light skin and a large gun.

"Sit down," the light-skinned soldier fumed as I stood there, paralyzed. "Sit down!" he repeated. The dark-skinned soldier pushed me from behind with his gun, once, then twice. Kayitesi stood up and extended her hands towards me.

"*Celi ngwino wicare iruhande rwanjye,*" she said. (Celi, come and sit by my side.) Trembling, I walked towards her and sat down beside her on the far end of the sofa.

The light-skinned soldier, who seemed to be the leader, was standing in the middle of the living room, looking furious. *"Ubwo rero mwashakaga gukiza aka kana ka kanyenzi mwanze kutubwira ko hari undi muntu mu nzu,"* he said, *"Kuri iyo mpamvu rero turabanza kwica aka kana tubakurikizeho."* (So, you lied that there was nobody else in the house. For that reason, we will start by killing this little girl before you.)

My heart lurched.

"Not my baby," Mum pleaded, rising to her feet in front of the soldier. "Not my children. Please, kill me and let them go. They are just children. Please let them go and kill me instead."

Her voice rose in desperation as she repeated herself over and over again.

"Shut up and sit down," the soldier roared, but she continued to beg the man.

"Please. Do not kill my children. Please kill me instead. Please kill me and let them go." Tears streamed down her cheeks, and her cries became increasingly shrill and panic-stricken. "Please!" she beseeched, "Please!"

Suddenly there was a deafening noise as the soldier fired his gun up into the ceiling. The sound of the shot was so terrifying that I grabbed my sister's hand, wanting her to hold me. The room began to fill with a strange odor that I could not place.

Mum stopped pleading and sat down. The air was thick with our terror. We all knew that we were going to die, and soon.

The dark-skinned soldier was holding a long list of names. The first two were crossed off with a red pen. The third name was my father's.

"Where's Murengezi Wilberforce?" he asked.

"He traveled to Zaire to bury his sister's husband," Mum replied.

"Ubwo yagiye kurwana hamwe n'inyenzi bene wanyu none urabeshya? Tura-

bica turabamara!" (You are lying. He probably went to the battlefront with the traitors. We will kill you all.)

Mum started negotiating. "We have money. I'll give you all of it, our two cars too. Take everything else you need as well, but do not touch my children."

The soldiers, taken aback by her determination and relentlessness, stepped into the kitchen for a brief meeting.

When they were out of sight, Claude began pleading with Mum. "Please, Mum, please stop shouting. It is making them angry."

"Yes Mum," said Kayitesi, "It's okay if they kill us. You said we are going to Heaven together, right?"

But Mum wasn't listening. Her eyes were full of tears, and I could not recognize her. I can only imagine that the thought of seeing her children die was unimaginable and unbearable for her.

The soldiers returned from the kitchen. "Okay, show us how much money you have, and what other valuables you own."

Mum opened her small purse that contained 25,000 Rwandan Francs (Rwf). She placed it on the coffee table. Claude dug into his pockets and brought out 6000 Rwf. Kayitesi removed her gold bracelet and dropped it on the table.

"This is not enough for us to spare even *one* traitor's life," the light-skinned soldier sneered after counting the money. "Give us more."

"We don't have any more," Mum said, adding, "But you won't touch my children!"

"We are taking the money and will kill you anyway," the soldier smirked.

Claude quickly offered up the keys to our two cars, but their minds were made up. The light-skinned soldier looked directly at Mum. "Since you lied in the beginning that there was nobody else in the house, we are going to kill the little one first, and then the rest of the children. You will be the last."

He raised his gun and pointed it at me. I grabbed my sister's hand and pulled myself close to her. As I moved, a shot rang out, and I felt the bullet whizz past my arm, penetrating the sofa.

Mum sprang back into action, "Please kill me first!" she said hysterically, "Please don't let me see my children die. I beg you. Be kind and kill me first!" She cried out, kneeling at his feet, holding the end of his gun, repeating the same words over and over again. Kayitesi attempted to pull her back, but Mum pushed her away. The soldier wrenched the gun out of her hands and smashed it over her head. I heard the sound of bone cracking. There was blood everywhere. "Sit down and shut up!" he screamed as the blood poured down Mum's face.

Claude quickly helped her up. She was semi-conscious and oblivious to the blood.

After a brief silence, the soldiers made their way back into the kitchen. It seemed Mum's response had destabilized them. Kayitesi used her scarf to wipe the blood from Mum's face. Once again, Claude pleaded with her not to shout. Mum was silent, but the determination on her face was resolute.

The soldiers returned from the kitchen. We cannot spare you. We have to kill all *inyenzi*[1] and government traitors. Your family is number three on the list of people who must be killed in this neighborhood."

"You have no right to kill my children," Mum responded fiercely.

I suddenly remembered the prayer that we had learned that morning and started reciting it in my head. I prayed the words five times, and I felt my fear dissipate. It was as if I was living in a dream. I saw Heaven —green grass, white robes, angels, Jesus, and mango trees—just like I had seen it in the children's books from church. It was as if I was already there. Everything felt so peaceful and joyful.

Crack! Another gunshot suddenly woke me from my dream. The room had fallen into a deathly silence. The soldiers were standing still, with one of their guns pointed at Mum. She appeared normal at a glance, but upon paying closer attention to her face, I could tell she was in a great deal of pain. She was gasping for air. After some time, she looked at the light-skinned soldier and said, "*Imana ibababarire*" (May God forgive you). The soldiers, taken aback by her comment, returned to the kitchen for a time. It seemed as if her statement had somehow made it difficult for them to execute their mission.

"Give us more money, and we'll leave you," they said when they came back, "But don't fool yourselves. You are going to die. It may not be today, but the next ones will kill you all for sure. We are sparing your lives today. Prepare to die tomorrow. Pray for God to welcome you. Be sure of this."

"Thank you," said Mum, "I have some money that I spared for my children. Let me go to my bedroom and find it for you."

"Hurry," said the soldier.

She tried to stand, wincing as she struggled to her feet, and then fell back onto the sofa. She tried and failed again. The light-skinned soldier pointed at Kayitesi: "*Muhagurutse di twihute.*" (Help her up quickly).With her arm on Mum's shoulder, Kayitesi helped her to stand. Her face was etched with pain. I noticed that she was limping, and she left a trail of blood on the floor as she moved.

We sat together quietly in the living room with the dark-skinned soldier, everyone looking at the blood on the floor. I still didn't understand what death meant, but I was becoming aware of the feelings that one has before dying. Fear, panic, nervousness, hopelessness, and desperation contorted together inside my chest.

When Mum returned, she was moving on one leg, limping, unable to step down on the floor with her bleeding foot. Her face was ashen. Kayitesi was crying. It was as if a sword were being slowly thrust through my heart.

"We are going for now," the light-skinned soldier reminded us, "but the next group that comes will kill you all, so be prepared for that."

They left, and our guard closed the gate.

Everyone gathered where Mum was seated. She was thirsty. Francine brought her water. I caught a glimpse of the wound on her foot. I had never seen such an injury before. Blood poured out in a steady stream. Mum asked for a cloth to cover the wound. Claude attempted to stop the bleeding. She directed him as she lay down on the sofa, gulping down several strong painkillers before closing her eyes.

My heart was heavy. I felt hopeless. I didn't know what to say or do. I took Mum's hands in my own, unable to hold back the tears that welled up in my eyes. Mum opened her eyes and looked at everyone. "I wish I could save you all," she said weakly, "I wish I could spare you the pain you are feeling."

A fever had crept in, and her face had become so pale that it was almost completely white. But, despite the pain and the fever, she mapped out a strategy of how we would spend the night. It was nearly 7:00 p.m. and it was dark outside. She told us that we were not going to sleep in the house because the soldiers may return. Instead, we would spend the night in the small bush outside. No lights were to be turned on, and no doors were to be closed. We were not to cook—we would eat leftovers from lunch, and prepare tea with bread. The house was to appear abandoned.

"Don't worry Celine," she said gently, "There are no snakes in the bush, and I will be by your side. Nothing will happen to you." Although I was terrified of snakes, that night, snakes mattered little to me. Seeing Mum's pallid complexion was far more terrifying. I asked myself why there was no plan to take her to the hospital to see a doctor, or to contact Mama Lily like we would do in the past whenever someone was sick.

Mum gave orders as we prepared to camp outside. She told us to wear two layers of clothes—something she had taught us since 1992[2]—and be ready to run if more soldiers came. Everyone was given a task. Françoise prepared tea. Claude brought warm bed covers. Kayitesi gathered food.

When we were ready, we entered the intimidating, dark bush, forming two groups. Francine, Mum and I hid at the entrance, and Kayitesi, Françoise, Beatrice (the house girl), and Claude crouched down in the middle.

It was a cold night. We could hear the sounds of people being shot throughout our neighborhood. *Rat-a-tat-tat-tat! Rat-a-tat-tat-tat!* And then silence. Bombs and grenades flew over our heads. I lay my head against Mum's chest, and she blanketed me with her arms, telling me not to worry and to try to get some sleep. But it was impossible to drift off for long. Everyone was either chanting their last prayers or being yanked back and forth between nightmares and reality. The constant explosions beat like drums in my ears until, eventually, silence descended around us.

Francine was sitting in the bush, unable to place her head on the grass. "Franci," Mum whispered, "lie here near me. Let Celine give you a little bit of space so that both of you can lay your heads on my chest and sleep." I remember thinking how courageous it was of her to think about our wellbeing when *she* was the one who needed urgent atten-tion. I remember touching her face during the night. She was burning up and was shivering.

Francine called Claude.

"Claude! Claude!" Francine whispered as loud as she could, "Mum is not well. She is shivering. Please come." Claude crept through the bush towards us with Kayitesi and Françoise.

"Call Mama Nina," said Mum, "Tell her what has happened and ask her for medicine for the fever and pain." Mama Nina, our neighbor, was a nurse. Her house was not far from ours, but, for the sake of keeping our voices low, Claude had to move between the bush and the fence of Mama Nina's property to convey our messages back and forth.

Claude crept out of our hiding place to call Mama Nina. We huddled around Mum. She was trembling. Despite her obvious pain, she tried to hide it, telling us not worry, that with some medicine she would be okay and that we must stay hidden in the bush. We waited quietly, but we were deeply concerned about her.

Claude returned. "Mama Nina says she'll come by the fence with medicine."

Within a few minutes, we heard Mama Nina's voice.

"Are you there? Mama John[3]," she whispered, "Are you there?"

"Yes," Kayitesi answered.

"How is the wound? What color is it?" Mama Nina asked.

Kayitesi turned her flashlight to shine on Mum's wound. It was seeping dark blood.

"I am going to give you some instructions," Mama Nina said, "You have to follow and do exactly what I say, okay?"

Kayitesi nodded. We could feel that Mama Nina was worried about Mum's fragile state.

Mama Nina passed a small box to Claude through the fence. "The contents are for the fever. Monitor her temperature and give her one pill every four hours. Tell Kayitesi to make sure that she cleans the wound using Mercurochrome."

It was difficult for me to make sense of what I was witnessing—Francine supporting Mum so that she sat up straight, Kayitesi cleaning the wound, and Claude, as the messenger, running to the fence for further instructions from Mama Nina, and returning to tell Kayitesi what to do. I was standing beside Françoise, shielded by the bush, holding her hand tightly. Mum was in so much pain. From the dim light of the torch, I could see it in her face, but she was trying to be strong and brave. I felt so hopeless, so empty, and so worried. I could not stop crying. Kayitesi had never seen such wounds or so much blood, yet she knew that she had to play the role of the family nurse. She was composed and quiet, doing exactly what Claude was telling her to do.

I don't know how long we all sat there as Mum's wound was dressed, but I vividly remember her pain. I remember thinking about Dad. I was thinking that had Dad been there with us, he would have done something to help us. He would have taken Mum to the hospital. He would have taken us to Nairobi where we had spent our summer holidays three years earlier. I suddenly longed to be in Heaven. I recalled the beautiful images I saw earlier that day when I was daydreaming. I remembered Jesus and the angels in their white robes. I told myself that when we finally all got to Heaven, it would be so much better than what I was seeing around me—Mum's blood, her face, the way she was shaking, my teenage siblings being doctors and nurses. Surely Heaven was safe, peaceful, and beautiful?

---

1. Cockroaches, or rebels
2. The liberation war in Rwanda began in 1990
3. In Rwanda, mothers are often called by the name of their first born child. In Mum's case, John was her first born child, hence Mama John.

6

The 8th Of April, 1994

*B*y the following morning, Mum was a little bit better. Everyone had returned to their camping spots, and the gunshots had subsided. Sleep was difficult. Francine was having a hard time finding a place to lie down, but she was quiet and patient. She was watching Mum and monitoring her fever. It was dawn, almost 6:00 a.m. We heard Mama Nina at the fence, telling Mum that people in the neighborhood were taking refuge at the nun's convent nearby and that we should all go there. Surely nobody will harm people at a holy place, especially children, said Mum hopefully. We agreed to leave immediately. Mum told us to grab a few necessities like blankets, layered clothing, and as much food as we could carry.

As we left the gate, we saw that the road was empty. It was bitterly cold. Mum was still limping, but she held onto Claude and Kayitesi for support. What should have been a ten-minute walk took us over thirty minutes. The nuns welcomed us warmly, and Mum was immediately given one of the nurse's rooms. The rest of us were ushered to the backyard. There were over one hundred and fifty people huddled there—many were families like ours. It was a sad and desperate sight. I looked at Kayitesi for support and encouragement as we joined the other refugees. She held my hands tightly in her own.

Our first night in the camp was strange for me. I was asked to sleep with other children of my age in one full room. I had never seen them before, and I refused to join them. I asked to stay with my sisters. It was one thing to be in a refugee camp with one hundred and fifty people in one house, but it was unimaginable to sleep separately from my family and in between strangers. The young adults slept on the terrace in front of the chapel and Kayitesi was my support throughout the night. Nobody spoke. The sound of bombs and gunshots filled the air. The fear around me was palpable.

We camped for two days in that fully packed compound. There was little to eat or drink. The nurses treated Mum, and Mum sent people to check on us and make sure that we were okay. We also went to check on her several times a day. She always smiled and made sure that we could feel her presence and her love. Her condition was improving, and she had regained some of her color and strength. While in her room, she would wrap her arms around me. I felt safe there. Her love, care, and encouragement made the refugee camp bearable.

On the 9th of April, we woke up at first light. It was cold outside on the terrace. The nuns had prepared porridge for everyone. My siblings and I went to check in on Mum and, to our surprise, she looked brighter and was even walking a bit. The fever had abated, and she was making every effort to stay up. I stayed with her the whole morning. Mum wanted me to go outside and play with the other children, but I refused. My heart was heavy, and I felt more attached to her than ever.

More people arrived at the convent that day. I wondered where they would all sleep—we were already so many. I remember the constant sound of babies crying. It was not home, and it was not fun, but Mum told me to be kind and patient, and portray a good attitude towards the nuns and other refugees. People were afraid and anxious, but families were trying to create a warm environment. Children played while the adults helped the nuns. Being there was bearable as long as I was there with my family and nothing separated us. Mum and my siblings were my refuge— my reason to live and not be afraid. There must have been about two hundred people there by the time darkness fell. We slept outside on the terrace again that night.

7

When Sunday Became
Dark Day

$\mathcal{I}$t was the tenth of April, 1994.

The sun rose on a hive of activity that Sunday morning. The nuns were making sure that everybody was ready for the church service. I ran to Mum who was still in her bedroom.

"Why aren't you in the chapel with others?" she asked, hugging me.

"I want to be with you, Mum," I replied.

"Okay then," she said, and smiled, "Help me get up."

When we arrived, people were praying, and the skies resounded with heavenly melodies. Suddenly, and out of nowhere, soldiers came storming into the compound. I don't recall exactly how many of them there were, but there were definitely more than five. Two of them positioned themselves on the terrace, with the others between the house and the gate, making sure that there was no escape route for us.

I wondered who they were, why they were shouting, and why they were so angry with us. I remembered the soldiers who attacked us at home three days earlier and the shot that wounded Mum. I thought about her prayer, that thing called 'death', Heaven, and Jesus.

The soldiers fired shots in the air and ordered everyone to leave the compound. They started shoving us so that we would move faster. When they were certain that everyone in sight was brought outside, including the nuns, they pointed to a small road that led to the main road and told us to walk. Mum held my hand. I looked up at her for encouragement and safety. Most of all, I looked to her for an explanation of what was going on. She looked so peaceful and composed. I searched for answers in my mind.

"Why are we going down there? What is there? Can the soldiers explain where they are taking us? Why are they so angry with everyone? What have we done? Is this the journey to Heaven? Is death down there? What does it look like? Why does death want to take all these people? Is Jesus waiting for us?"

I was confused, thoughts whirling around in my head. Seeing Claude helping Mum as she walked, Francine coming to hold my hand, and Mum's serenity calmed my restless mind.

Everyone walked down the road in silence. We were the last group to arrive at the main road. It was there that I saw death.

Death was in the form of people. Death was standing there, waiting for us. There were about fifty men (there may have been women among them, but I could not tell) wearing clothes and headdresses made of banana leaves. They were armed with blood-stained machetes and other strange looking weapons made of wood and metal. Their clothes were drenched in blood. The looks on their faces were diabolical and terrifying. Death was real. Death was unlike anything that I could have imagined. Death spoke clearly without uttering a word. It was in that moment that I finally understood what Death was, and Mum's prayer began to make sense to me. The time for death had come.

8

Separation

$\mathcal{I}$t was around 10:00 a.m. We were ordered to sit down in the middle of the dusty road. People reached out to each other for comfort.

A few soldiers approached us and shouted, "If you know you are a Hutu and you are among these *Inyenzi*, get out and save yourselves. There's no need to die with traitors."

Those with a Hutu ID stood up immediately and showed the soldiers their papers before being released and making their way back up the hill.

I could hear Mum pleading with Françoise. "Get up. Save yourself. Go in peace, my daughter."

Françoise was a Hutu, but she shook her head. "I am not leaving you here," she cried. "Where will I go? What will I become? Why do you have to die? You have been so good to me."

She held on to Mum tightly, refusing to leave us there. "If you are to die, then I will die too."

A soldier who stood nearby heard a piece of the conversation and asked what was happening.

Mum pushed Françoise to her feet. "Please spare her," she pleaded with the soldier, "She is a Hutu and must not be killed. Please."

The soldier asked Françoise for her ID.

"Woman!" he shouted, examining her papers, "What are you waiting for? Get up and leave these *Inyenzi*. Go find refuge. You don't deserve to die."

Françoise sat back down in silence and looked away. "You!" spat the soldier angrily, "Get up!"

Françoise looked into his eyes fearlessly, with courage and determination. "Yes," she said. "I am Hutu. But this is my mother and my family. If you kill them, you will have to kill me too."

The soldier, confused, hesitated for a moment and then laughed. "You are a fool. Let your wish be granted. You will die as painfully as they will."

The tension was overwhelming. I was grappling to understand what was happening. The only certainty was that death had arrived.

A soldier's voice reverberated loudly through the crowds of people. "*Abana tuzabasasira umubyeyi.*" (We shall lay our parent's [Habyarimana] grave with the children's corpses.)

"Nuns," he commanded, "Take back the little children with you. We will come back for them and the other *Inyenzi* among you. Children, go back to the convent. Hurry!"

Anguished cries rang out as mothers said their final goodbyes to their children and handed them over to the nuns. The children, in tears, asked why they were being sent away, but there were no answers. The scene was one of heartbreaking chaos. I remained seated. It was as if the soldier was speaking to every other child except me. To me, his words were irrelevant. The message did not fit. My mind did not and could not comprehend what he was saying. Children walked back up the hill in slow motion. Mum was looking at me strangely. I could not understand why she was hugging me so tightly and why my sisters were smiling at me with tears in their eyes. I was screaming inside, wishing that everybody would stop acting so strangely.

Returning to my senses, I heard my family say goodbye to me. It took me a few seconds to understand what they were doing, the meaning of their actions. They were telling me to go along with the other children —to go and find refuge at the convent with the nuns. They were sad, but they were hopeful for my life. "Maybe you will survive, Celine. Maybe you will tell Johnny and the others what happened."

"No Mama! No!" I sobbed, "What are you saying? You promised. You promised we'd be together. You promised we would go to Heaven together. You promised we would see Jesus. No Mama! I'm not going back unless we go together! Why do you want to leave me? Why are you not all coming with me? Why can't I come with you?"

I continued crying out to Mum, but she would not respond. I let go of her *kitenge*[1] and reached out to Kayitesi, grabbing at her pullover and holding it tight, sobbing, and asking why they were not coming with me, over and over again. Claude tried to reason with me, but it was in vain. I was resolute.

"No Mama!" I insisted, "We are either all going back, or we are staying here together!"

I could not fathom why my siblings and my Mum wanted to send me away from them to an unknown place, to be alone with complete strangers. The thought of being all on my own without my family was beyond frightening.

I was wailing so much that my whole family began sobbing. The situation was chaotic and hopeless. The irony of the dilemma was impossible to untangle. Eventually, I grew weary from the heavy tears of desperation, and my voice became hoarse. "Please, Mum, I beg you," I pleaded, one last time, "Don't leave me. I beg you."

It was terrifying and heart wrenching to see my family giving me away as if they no longer wanted me to go to Heaven with them. I couldn't understand what wrong I had committed to deserve this.

"It's the best thing to do," Mum reassured me. I had never heard her speak with such piercing clarity. "I will be very happy if you obey me and go back with the nuns." My heart sank to my knees. I was disoriented and started shaking from all the crying. I continued to resist until I had no strength left in me. But I held my position firmly, determined to die with my family. I had been prepared for that by "the prayer".

In the meantime, other children were going up in groups. Families were saying their goodbyes, but there was not enough time for these goodbyes. The soldiers were in a hurry, urging children to go back quickly. "Hurry!" they shouted, "We need to start the work." The *Interahamwe* group was standing in the same place as before, observing, making sure that no grown-ups escaped. Their eyes were evil. Their clothes were full of blood, and they were holding their machetes ready to "*start the work*".

Mum, realizing that she was running out of time to save me, pulled my elder sister Francine towards me. "Here! Go with Francine. You won't be alone. Go with her and both of you will be saved. Don't worry. You will stay with her. She will protect you." She looked at me sternly, making it clear that there was no other option: I was to go back to the convent without Mum—without the rest of my family. She reached out into her bag and said, "Take these keys and give them to Johnny when he comes back from Kenya. They are the house keys and the car keys. Don't lose them." She sighed deeply and said, "Celine. Be a good girl. Obey the nuns. Now go with Francine." She then pushed me towards the path to the convent.

Francine grasped my hand and pulled me away. I started walking backwards slowly, looking at Mum, Kayitesi, Claude, and Françoise. I could not believe what my eyes were seeing. "They're staying?" I asked myself, "Will they come back for me?" I was hoping that Mum would change her mind in those final seconds, but instead, she encouraged me with a smile, her eyes full of tears, trying her best to keep herself together for me. I was confused and deeply hurt by her betrayal.

A few meters away, an *Interahamwe* with a particularly terrifying face stopped us in our tracks, pushing Francine away from me.

"Where do you think you are going?" he roared, "Are you a child? Look at you! Look at your breasts." He lifted her left breast with a machete, laughing and showing it off to the other *Interahamwe* nearby. "Look at this *inyenzi*," he sneered, "She thinks she is still a child with such breasts. She could be nursing one of the *inyenzi*."

They all laughed.

I was paralyzed. I looked at the humiliation on Francine's face. The *Interahamwe* pushed her away telling her, "Go back with the others. You are not a child anymore. You deserve to die."

Mum pleaded with the *Interahamwe* from where she sat, "Please, let her go too. She is still a child. She just grew up quickly. She is the older sister to that little one. Please let her be safe."

The *Interahamwe* laughed, shoving Francine in Mum's direction. "Go back quickly," he jeered, "You are dying today." His voice was angry and laced with self-satisfaction. Francine turned around silently, adjusted her clothes and made her way back. I watched as Mum threw her arms around Francine protectively. I was paralyzed with fear and confusion, not knowing where to go or what to do. My legs were heavy, and I was unable to move. My world as I knew it was over.

I was among the last of the children remaining on the main road when the others climbed back up the hill towards the convent. I watched as the nuns and the older children, who were more than six to ten years old, carried the babies. I was stuck in between the hill and my family. I looked back at Mum, who motioned with her hands for me to go up the hill.

I heard a voice behind me saying, "Let's go, dear." It was one of the nuns. She took my hand and pulled me to start walking up the hill with her. Her comforting voice was all I needed to succumb. I looked back at my family and then turned and walked up the hill.

As we walked up the hill, I looked back to see if they were still there. The *Interahamwe* was gathering everyone together and steering them towards the gate of a nearby house. I saw one of them beating Claude, forcing him to move forward. I stopped walking for a second, but the nun pulled me up again, and we continued. When we arrived at the top of the hill, I turned to look again, but my family was out of sight. I entered the convent and joined the other children who were gathered together in a small room.

---

1. African fabric

9

The Orphanage, Our New Home

I was still seated at my favorite spot in the living room, downloading the memories into my diary. A strange, warm sensation suddenly began to spread across my head as I recalled the details of their gruesome deaths. I felt myself gasping for air. I heard the screams, the prayers, and the supplications, but it was all too much to bear. I clutched my head with both my hands and bowed down into my knees as I tried to shut the voices out, but it was in vain. I stood up, rushed to my bedroom, and turned on the radio. Soft gospel music was playing.

"Help me, God. Help me," I cried. I felt as if I was losing my mind. I cried until I passed out.

I did not show Gilbert my notes or reveal what I had experienced that afternoon when he returned home that evening. He was completely unaware of what I was going through.

I picked up my notebook a few days later, this time with a renewed sense of strength to continue. I wanted to tell Mum what had happened after we were separated.

Dear Mum,

I wish I never learned of the horrible death you experienced. No words can express how the 10th of April, 1994, destroyed my life and how it injured my heart and my soul. My inner self always wished that, if only this date could be erased from history, that maybe none of this would have ever happened to you.

Right after we reached the convent, we were taken into a tiny room. The children were all very quiet. Nobody ran around or played. It was around 11:00 a.m. We had not eaten breakfast, but no one felt hungry. The atmosphere was strange and heavy.

There were around thirty-five children in the room, and the only voices heard in the room were the cries of the babies. The rest of us were disoriented, confused, and hopeless. You could sense the questions in their little brains, "Where is my family? What are they doing to them? What is going to happen to us? Is my family coming back for me?"

Everyone was lost, unable to make sense of the separation and pain while imagining our loved ones being hacked and stabbed to death with machetes and knives. We could hear the bombs and grenades around us.

The nuns brought us food around 1:00 p.m. It was rice and sauce, or beans—I think. I was unable to eat. My heart was so heavy that the smell of the food was almost unbearable. I stared at the door in the hope of seeing one of you appear to take me to be with you.

At 2:00 p.m., we heard a group of people entering the main gate. The voices grew louder as they came closer to our room. We thought it was our families coming back for us, but it was the *Interahamwe* who had just finished killing you. There was blood all over their bodies. Their traditional wooden weapons and machetes were covered in blood as well. They spoke proudly of how they killed you.

"You kids," they said, "We will come for you tomorrow. We will kill you too. You are children of *inyenzi* and deserve to die like your parents. We killed them all."

They laughed amongst themselves, gloating sickeningly over how easy it was to kill *inyenzi* traitors. I was terrified and sick with the horror of seeing your blood all over them.

I watched as they left the room, still laughing and proud of themselves. Sitting in my corner, I bowed my head between my knees. I felt nauseous and dizzy. My little brain could not fathom how I was with you a moment ago, and the next you were no more. Were you really gone without me? I went back to the room where you were sleeping a few hours ago to look for you—to double check and see that you had not returned. But the room was empty and cold.

I found a piece of your *kitenge*. It had blood on it from the shot to your foot. I picked it up carefully and walked back to the small room where the other children were, holding onto it tightly. I saw a corner in the room and went to sit there quietly. I told myself that if I held it and kept it safe that you would come back—that you would be happy and proud of how responsible I was.

The days that followed your death on the 10th of April were empty and purposeless. I lost all sense of time. Nothing made sense anymore. My heart jumped every time a door opened, only to find that it wasn't you. I would comfort my soul with your *kitenge*. I refused to wash your blood from it or allow the other children to use it.

The convent had become an orphanage—our new home. The same group of *Interahamwe* would visit us every day with the same torturous message: "We will kill you too. Be prepared." We lived in a state of perpetual fear, waiting for our imminent deaths.

The nuns continued to welcome in more children. One day a four-year-old old girl was brought in. Her name was Dany. Her hands had been shot, and there were gaping wounds where the bullets had entered. The person who found her said that she was lying with her family— they had all been shot dead.

The nuns took great care of us. They were not prepared to run an orphanage with so many needs, but God bless their souls. They gave us shelter, white rice, and beans to eat, and sometimes water to drink. The number of children grew to more than thirty-five, with many of them under the age of five. The nuns chose four of us who were between the ages of ten and twelve to take care of the little ones. I was accustomed to being taken care of as the last born at home, but my life had changed dramatically—nothing would ever be the same. I remembered the last instruction you gave me—to obey the nuns. I took the responsibility seriously, and looked forward to receiving your praise for a job well done.

The *Interahamwe* returned to the convent one day after another with the same message: "You are going next. You will be our last Tutsis to kill. It is only a matter of days."

One day, they arrived with soldiers armed with guns, machetes, and knives and ordered all the orphans to get out of the room and form a line on the terrace. The younger children started crying from fear and distress, so we picked them up and hurried outside. We were told to line up so that we could be shot. One girl, Mireille Kagabo, who looked a bit older than us, was shoved to the ground in the middle of the compound and a gun was pointed at her head. We were terrified. The babies were crying, and the nuns pleaded hysterically for our lives. But the soldiers were determined to shoot Mireille in front of us, and then kill us one at a time right there where we stood in line.

I remembered the prayer you taught us. I closed my eyes and repeated the prayer many times as I prepared to be shot dead.

I understood that if they killed me as they killed you, then I would come to you in Heaven. I hoped that you were looking for a way to come back and take me with you.

But something had changed since I started taking care of the babies among us. I developed an attachment to them. I began to fear for their lives. They didn't deserve to die. Because they needed my protection, I was torn between my strong desire to join you and my siblings and the strong urge to continue protecting the babies.

I guess God made the choice for me. As I stood there, my eyes closed, reciting the prayer over and over again in my heart, I heard the soldiers order us to go back to the room. They told us that they would return to finish the job the following day. I didn't understand what just happened—it was just another miracle.

Life in the convent meant hiding in the small bedroom, covering the window with mattresses at all times in case a grenade, a bomb, or a bullet found its way in. Taking care of the little ones meant ensuring that they ate their food, and accompanying them to the one metallic bucket that we all used as a toilet. The smell of the bucket was insufferable, and the nuns took us one by one, teaching us how to clean up afterward. We had to move quickly because the toilet was outside in the open. There were bullets and grenades flying over our heads and all around us. There were some days where it was too dangerous to venture out, and we would have to hold it in. This was bearable for the older children but difficult for the little ones. Sometimes the shooting was so bad that we would spend two days indoors and it was forbidden to go out for any reason, even to use the toilet. There were no nappies for the babies, and without access to the metal bucket outside, they had no choice but to relieve themselves in their clothes.

Most of the times the circumstances were all too much for us. Little children would start crying, calling for their parents, asking the nuns where their families were, and whether they were coming back. To keep the situation under control, the nuns had to be tough on us, especially those of us who were older. We had to learn how to comfort the younger children while we were crying our own silent tears. At ten years old, I was the mother to four children.

Bombs and grenades fell into the compound constantly. One day, a grenade exploded on the terrace in front of our room. Another day, a canister of tear gas was thrown into our room and the gas spread throughout the compound; it was terrifying. There was so much smoke that we could not see where we were going. Our eyes stung from the gas and everyone was running and screaming. The smell was suffocating. This became a daily routine and we had no choice but to accept it.

The risk of stray grenades or bullets killing us was our everyday reality, but we had to remain calm and stay indoors as much as possible.

We left Kigali one month after your death, but little did we know that life in the convent was quite tolerable compared to what lay ahead of us.

10

From The Convent To The Refugee Camp

*A*lthough the nuns took great care of us and did everything they could to ensure that we were safe, we were not safe and food was becoming scarce. The nuns told us that Kicukiro, where the convent was situated, was right in the middle of the war zone between the hills.

After the terrace was bombed, one of the nuns, Louise, left to seek help from a nearby clergy house so that we could be moved to a safer place in Kabgayi. Upon meeting with the priests there, she was introduced to two kind-hearted soldiers from the former *Force d'armée rwandaise*, Samuel and Rukundo. The soldiers returned to the convent two days later, bringing Louise with them, much to the nuns' relief—they thought she had been killed along the way.

Samuel asked the nuns to open the windows. "The windows can't block the bullets. Let the children get some fresh air."

"We have to go, but we'll be back soon," Rukundo, reassured the nuns, "Don't worry."

They returned a few days later with more soldiers. Rukundo gave one of the nuns strict instructions: "I don't want anyone to carry anything with them. Wake the children up, bring them all out, and we'll tell you what to do next. And also, don't lock up the house. We'll leave it as it is. If the *Interahamwe* return and think that the house is still occupied, they won't send the others to find and kill us. Hopefully, we will have covered some ground before they come after us."

We were told to pack up our belongings. We were restricted to taking a set of clothes that we would wear for a long time without changing, a bed sheet if we had one, and a pair of shoes—nothing more. We were to move early in the morning.

It felt surreal walking away from the convent that day. The soldiers told us to move in a single file line and to stop in our tracks and immediately fall to the ground when we heard gunshots.

We were running for our lives, like frightened zombies. In the trenches to the left and right of us were bodies lying in pools of blood.

I found myself in the familiar surroundings of my neighborhood. I looked for our home and all I could see were plumes of black smoke rising from where the roof used to be. My heart sank. I stood there, statuesque, the other children silent, each experiencing a similar loss. In a matter of weeks, families had been replaced with communities of refugees, and mattresses with cold, hard floors. A feeling of utter hopelessness consumed me. "My family's gone. My home is gone. This is surely the end of the world." But we had to keep moving.

We were loaded onto pickups and mini trucks that were waiting for us. We would drive from Kigali to Gitarama, a small town in the south. After driving for about an hour down Mont Kigali, in Butamwa, we ran into a roadblock at the Nyabarongo River. It was full of *Interahamwe* and soldiers armed with guns. They motioned for us to stop.

"Get out of the vehicles," they shouted.

Rukundo and Samuel stepped out and walked towards them.

"Where are you taking them?" the *Interahamwe* asked.

Rukundo handed them a document[1]. "We have been instructed to transport them to Kabgayi. They are to reach there safely."

"Impossible!" the *Interahamwe* snorted, "Those children are cock-roaches. We know that some of you soldiers are spies. Bring those snakes so we kill them!"

They refused to allow us to pass. The roadblock was there to kill any Tutsi who tried to escape, without exception. We were orphans because our parents were Tutsi, and that meant that we had to die too.

"Get them out!" they shouted, motioning to Samuel and Rukundo to remove us from the vehicles, "We will throw the cockroaches into the river and feed them to the crocodiles!"

Rukundo and Samuel eventually threatened to shoot their way through the roadblock if the Interahamwe refused to comply.

"Listen," said one of the *Interahamwe* to another, "They have a signed document with specific orders. We will cause trouble for ourselves if we engage with them. Let them go."

We traveled as far off the main road as we could after that, using short-cuts that cut through green banana plantations to rural areas that were less dangerous. We encountered more roadblocks. Rukundo, Samuel and the other soldiers, afraid but brave, protected us, persistently negotiating safe passage, telling the *Interahamwe* that we were ordinary orphans from a nearby orphanage and that we had lived there for a long time.

At every roadblock, we watched with horror as captured Tutsis, including children, were beaten and hacked to death. The road was littered with corpses. Life became increasingly incomprehensible with every death that we witnessed, and the trauma inside me became all-consuming.

It was around 6:00 p.m. when we reached the school in Kabgayi. We were exhausted, hungry, and terrified as we were led to the classroom in which we would spend the night. When we woke the following morning, we discovered that we were in a refugee camp with about twelve thousand other people. It was the first time I had ever seen so many people in one place.

It was a miracle that we had reached safely, but we were not out of danger. Groups of *Interahamwe* frequently visited the camp, going through every classroom, identifying every Tutsi man, woman, boy, and girl, and then returning in the dark to capture them. The nights would be filled with the screams of people being beaten and killed.

We were identified as *"Za nzoka z'i Kigali."*[2], followed by the words *"Mwebwe tuzabasasira umubyeyi"*[3] The *Interahamwe* arrived at the camp daily, dressed in bloodstained clothes, to remind us that our bodies would be used to line the grave of Habyarimana. Knowing that a horrible death awaited us at any given moment left us in a state of perpetual fear and mental anguish, wishing that we were already dead.

We spent the month of May in the packed refugee camp. It was filthy and unhygienic. Food became scarce, and we often found ourselves drifting through days on end without a meal. When food arrived, we would desperately shove and squeeze our way through the crowd of twelve thousand other adults and children, scrambling for a handful of beans that would have to sustain us for at least another week.

There were no toilets, so we relieved ourselves in the bush. Our days were spent in survival mode—we were not really living. We explored the hills in search of food and water, risking our lives, knowing that we might encounter *Interahamwe* and be killed. We would come across the bloody, lifeless bodies of the people we had heard screaming for their lives the night before, tossed into trenches and holes that had been dug in the ground. I had never seen so many dead people in my life, but with the numbing power of time, jumping over or walking around these bodies became quite normal.

Our primary source of water was the swamp—it was far from safe, but it was all we had. Once, after scooping some water into my bowl and drinking thirstily, I stopped to look down and discovered something resting at the bottom of my bowl. It was a pale blue human finger. I instinctively tossed the bowl away, the water spilling to one side, the finger flying to the other, and, along with the other children, ran back to camp. By then, I had become a zombie. I no longer screamed at the sight of a dismembered human body part. But hell was dragging me deeper into its pit, inch by inch, ripping away pieces of my already-broken soul.

Our hair and clothes were infested with lice. Many of us contracted diarrhea, and some never survived. I remember a four-year-old girl named Ines, who, despite her empty stomach, vomited continuously. We kept her hydrated with water, adding salt and sugar on lucky days, but she eventually succumbed to her illness. As for the rest of us, we had no other choice but to continue living in the squalor, risking our lives again the next day if we were to make it through another.

One morning, I remember heading out with my companions from the city in search of sweet potatoes, following the children who lived in the rural areas. The rural children laughed at us, making fun of our igno-rance, refusing to harvest the sweet potatoes for us when we asked them. Being from Kigali city, we had never harvested anything before, but we learned to do it ourselves, eating them raw. Being born into a middle working class family, many of my fellow refugees saw me as *umutesi*,—a "pampered" child. I felt like I had no place in this life.

One day, we came upon a plantation of African eggplants—vegetables that I had never been fond of, even today. It had been three weeks since we last ate a proper meal, but despite my overwhelming hunger, I was unable to indulge in the raw feast. I later spotted an area where I found four-leaf clovers growing—I recognized them from the time we spent at my grandparents. I remembered how we were always getting into trouble for gleefully sucking on the salt these plants had to offer. Finding something familiar to eat was such a relief that I returned to the area daily to indulge in the clovers for the remainder of that month.

The prayer that Mum had taught us the morning of the seventh of April, before the soldiers came, had prepared me to die and go to Heaven. I was looking forward to it. And yet, here I was—alive, but alone. I pleaded to God, asking Him why Mum had left me behind. Could my family not see me suffering? Did they not love me? I wondered whether Jesus had not perhaps forbidden them from taking me with them. I asked myself what I had done wrong to have been rejected and abandoned by my family like this.

---

1. The soldiers had asked their supervisor to draft and sign this document prior to our departure. Without it, we would have surely been killed.
2. The snakes from Kigali
3. We shall line our parent's (Habyarimana) grave with your corpses

11

Inkotanyi - Rwandan Patriotic Front (RPF)

*O*n the night of the first of June, 1994, we heard a commotion outside. Many people were suddenly on the move, and the sound of roaring car engines filled the night sky. Nobody could explain what was happening.

On the morning of the second of June, I woke up to the sound of bullets and bombs—the same sounds that marked my first day in Hell —but this time there were more than before. Looking around the camp in confusion, I spotted dark figures that dotted the top of the hill ahead of me. I recognized them as soldiers, but they were unfamiliar. They wore different uniforms to the ones we were used to seeing. There were no *Interahamwe* around.

At 11:00 a.m. these unfamiliar soldiers approached us. There was something different about their demeanor. They looked human. There were no verbal threats. They were friendly. There were refugees in our camp who recognized these soldiers. They were known as the *Inkotanyi*[1]. They hurriedly asked us if there were any wounded or sick among us, and then told us to prepare to move to Ruhango, a nearby town that was well-secured by the Rwandan Patriotic Front (RPF).

They reassured us that our lives were no longer in danger—that we were safe.

The crowd went hysterical, cheering, clapping, and shouting praises. Although I still felt quite numb, for the first time in a long time, there was hope in the faces and voices of the people around me. The dark spirit of agony that had settled and made its home in the camp was replaced with a spark of hope for life.

We were still in the middle of the battlefield and had to vacate the camp as quickly as possible to give the *Inkotanyi* room to continue advancing towards the enemy. We ran as fast as we could down the hill, many with their belongings. Some even took their cows with them. I fell hard while running past a cemetery and cried out in pain as a small, sharp, wooden crucifix pierced my leg. It was lodged in so deeply that I was unable to pull it out, and I continued running until we reached the main road at the bottom of the hill. One of the ladies that I had spent much of my time with at the refugee camp tended to my injured leg, pulling the crucifix out and covering my bleeding wound with her head wrap.

Over the next three days, I limped the fifty kilometers to Ruhango. There was little food or water, and the journey was arduous. The group of thirty-five of us from Kigali had developed a strong familial bond, and we knew that if we rested for too long, we risked getting lost in the crowd and becoming separated from each other. We had to take care of the younger children as we endured the hills. We slept under the dark sky and were soaked to the bone when it rained two of the nights. To make matters worse, I lost my Mum's *kitenge*. I was hysterical, and everybody looked at me as if I had gone crazy when I asked them whether they had seen it, but I didn't care. It was all I had left of her, and it was gone. I could feel the morphine that had numbed my heart slowly wearing off—the glaring reality of the impact of the Genocide consuming me from the inside out.

It was in Ruhango that I first experienced life in a hut. We joined another refugee camp there, where people had built huts for shelter. Some were unoccupied, and we claimed them for ourselves. We found a tin of Nido—a powdered milk that we were all so fond of in our childhood—in the first hut that we entered. Ravenous, the sight was nothing short of a miracle—a gift from heaven. We stared at it in awe for a moment before rushing towards it, eating it dry. We ate so much of it that we were sick to our stomachs.

The conditions at the Ruhango refugee camp were far better than those at Kabgayi. We felt secure, with RPF, UNICEF and other NGOs present. We were given biscuits called compact and triangular milk biscuits that contained the necessary nutrients we so desperately needed. Dehydrated and listless, we were given water solutions containing sugar to drink. There was medical care, and there was food.

We were given one portion of food per day—a handful of rice. The first time I queued up at mealtime with twenty thousand others, a large spoon of hot rice was ladled into my hands. Unprepared for the searing heat, I dropped it to the ground. That was it—my meal for the day had been wasted, lying in the dirt for the insects and the birds to enjoy later on when the crowds had dispersed. Thierry Kagabo, one of the thirty-five children from the orphanage in Kigali, graciously gave me his compact biscuit after seeing what had happened. I survived on that biscuit for the rest of the day. The following day, and for the rest of my stay in Ruhango, I learned to endure those first few seconds of heat. If I was to eat, I had no choice but to toughen up.

***

It was in Ruhango that the fog in my head began to clear. The daily anticipation of death slowly faded away, and I started to think about my situation. It felt as though my childhood had been ripped from beneath me and there was an overwhelming sense of obligation to grow up and to take care of myself.

One morning, after eating, I went to sit on top of a mound of dirt in the middle of the refugee camp. It was elevated high above the ground, offering a view of the entire camp. I sat there silently, watching what was going on below me, and realized that out of the twenty thousand people there, I knew no one personally—including the children I had met at the convent in Kicukiro. I saw families walking together and siblings sitting together. I saw happy people. I saw people celebrating. I was suddenly overcome with a sense of devastating loneliness. I had nobody, and I had nothing to celebrate. Sitting in the middle of the camp at the top of that mound, life was utterly meaningless and sorrowful.

---

1. The RPF soldiers, or Inkotanyi, were fighting a freedom war against the government in power, while also helping people from being killed.

12

The Reunion

*S*everal days later, a unit of UNICEF in charge of reuniting families started registering all the refugees in the camp. When my turn came, I stood there like a zombie—my heart numb, and my face emotionless as I gave the man on the other side of the desk the details he asked for. He asked me for my father's name. I looked at his name tag. *Serge Rwamasirabo*, it read.

"Murengezi Wilberforce," I replied.

"Mmh? *Nde* (Who)?" He stopped writing, visibly surprised, and asked me again.

"Murengezi Wilberforce," I repeated.

"Are you sure?" he asked again, unable to hide the shock on his face.

I stood there numbly and nodded.

"And what is your mother's name?" the man asked.

"Mukeshimana Norah."

He dropped his pen and stared at me before getting up from his seat and rushing around the table towards me and hugging me tightly. I stood there in his arms, stiff and confused. Although I had no desire to be embraced by a complete stranger, I felt something—I felt *seen*.

"You are the one who survived?" he asked, looking at me again.

"Yes."

"Celine, your father is looking for you. He is alive," he said.

Alive? I was skeptical. As far as I was concerned, my father had been killed at the border, and my older brother, Johnny, was at university in Nairobi where he had been studying since 1993. I had accepted it in my heart that I would never see my family again. I did not even expect to be reunited with Johnny. Those three months felt like ten years, and I had accepted that I was alone.

The news hit a wall. His words made no sense to me.

"I am a friend of your father," he said, "Your father is not dead. He is in Nairobi."

He reached for a pen and a piece of paper and placed it down on the table in front of me. "Write him a letter. Your father knows that one of his children survived, and he has been looking for you."[1]

I was so numb that I was unable to receive the news. I felt no joy. I felt no emotion at all. He put the pen in my hand. "Please, Celine," he insisted, "Please write to your father. He has already lost so much hope. He has started to believe that the news of your survival is false."

I held the pen tightly and pulled the piece towards me. I would write the letter so that my father would believe I was alive.

Hello Dad. It's Celine. Mum died. Kayitesi died. Claude died. Francine died. I stayed at a camp in Ruhango. Send me toothpaste and underwear. Bye.

That was it—I was too traumatized to see life any differently.

I walked back into the camp. Serge Rwamasirabo reached out to his network of contacts. Later that day, the nuns gathered us together and transported us to an orphanage at a refugee camp in Bugesera. I met a woman there who used to work with my mother. Recognizing me, she contacted Gratien, a colleague of my father and a friend of our family who had fled to Bugesera before we arrived there; she told him that a child from my family had survived. He came to find me immediately, hugging me tightly when he was brought to me. Gratien asked for my release from the orphanage, claiming to be an extended family member. I lived with him and his family in one of the abandoned houses in Bugesera for a while.

Although they took great care of me, my heart was locked away deep inside my chest. From the outside, I appeared to be fine, but nothing brought me joy. I was lost, suspended in the vast and empty void of something that I did not yet understand.

We later moved to a refugee camp in Byumba. This camp was considered the safest and furthest place from the war and killing. It had been under the control of the RPF for some time, and was far more organized than the previous camps I had stayed in—plus, there was food available. It was there that Gratien discovered that my cousins' family, the Nkubitos, were there, and all but one had survived. He took me to them and I was placed in their care. This was the first time since I was separated from my family that I was among people who were familiar to me outside of the orphanage—they were happy to see me and I was well taken care of during the time I stayed with them.

Not long after being welcomed into their home, news of my survival reached my aunt Therese who had also fled to the Byumba refugee camp. She came to see me immediately and we spent time together every day after that.

Meanwhile, my letter had reached Nairobi, in Kenya. Serge had given it to a friend of his in Kabale, Uganda, who had then sent it to Dad's friend, Aimable, in Nairobi.

Dad later told me the story of my letter:

There was a phone call.

"I have a letter for you from your child," said the voice at the end of the line.

"My child?" Dad asked. Since the Genocide began, my father had searched in vain for news of his surviving children.

"Yes," said the man on the other end of the line, "The letter is signed by Celine." Dad's hands were shaking as he tried to absorb the news.

"I have to rush to work," said the man, "But I'll leave it at home for you. You can come for it anytime."

When my father arrived, his friend's wife was there to welcome him. She handed him the letter. He read it, returned home, and then reread it with Johnny.

"Let's go and get her," they both decided. They sent a message to the Nkubitos to let them know that they were on their way. Communication at the time was basic and time-consuming, with messages often taking days, if not weeks, to reach the other side.

Dad and Johnny travelled to Kampala, the capital of Uganda, to see if there was a way for them to cross over the border into Rwanda. They spent the morning applying for special permission to be enter Rwanda, but the border officials were reluctant to let them cross the border—at the time, Rwanda was still not safe. Only aid workers were being allowed through. Refusing to give up, but also realizing that they might not be able to enter Rwanda, they sent a message to Aunt Therese, asking her to try to negotiate our passage over the border into Uganda. We would meet them at a restaurant in Kabale, a Ugandan town about four hundred and twenty kilometers south of Kampala.

It was not long after this message was sent that Dad and Johnny were granted special permission to cross the border into Rwanda. Unsure of whether their message had reached my Aunt Therese, they travelled to Byumba to find me. At the same time, Aunt Therese and I had reached the border post, and we were granted permission to cross into Uganda. Dad and Johnny, and Aunt Therese and I, crossed the border in opposite directions at almost the same time, completely missing each other.

When my father and brother reached Byumba, they were told that we had already left for Kabale, and so they turned around and began their trip back to Uganda.

The first things I asked for when we arrived at the restaurant in Kabale were fries and Coca-Cola. As I sat there drinking the very beverage that I had been prohibited to drink at home, Dad and Johnny walked in. I stayed seated as Aunt Therese stood up and went to hug them. They just stood there staring at me, and I back at them, none of us moving towards the other, nobody saying a word. Aunt Therese broke the long silence by telling me to go greet my father.

I rose from my seat and made my way to my father's arms. He hugged me and wept for what seemed like an eternity, mixed emotions of relief, joy, and anguish flooding through his body. Johnny silently, but tearfully embraced me. I was as emotionless as I was motionless. Incapable of responding, I went back to my seat and continued to eat my fries and drinking my bottle of Coca-Cola.

It was all surreal. After three months of not knowing from one day to the next when it would be my turn to be butchered to death, I was completely dead inside. Those three months felt like years, and, even though the Genocide was over, I was unable to comprehend what normal life was like. Psychologically, I was unable to recognize the feelings of joy and sorrow that my father and Johnny were expressing when they held me that day. I was emotionally numb.

---

1. My father was told that one of his younger children had survived, but he did not know whether it was me or Francine.

13

Nairobi

$\mathcal{W}$e spent the night in Kabale before continuing and, on 4th July 1994, the war ended.

My father, cognizant of my trauma, but unsure of how deep it ran, decided to send me to Nairobi with Johnny and join us there at a later date. He wanted to give me a chance to rest, rather than to return to what remained of our war-torn country. While Johnny and I traveled to Kenya (my father owned a four-bedroom apartment there), Dad headed to Kigali to begin the process of rebuilding a life for what was left of our family.

During the Genocide, one of our paternal uncles, Ndamukunda Wesley, had managed to escape Rwanda with his wife and five young children. When they had safely crossed over into Kenya, they were met by my father, who took them to live in his apartment with him and Johnny in Nairobi.

I spent four months in Nairobi. When asked about the Genocide, I told my cousins that my family had been killed and that we had moved around four different refugee camps before Dad and Johnny found me. Nobody dared to ask me about anything more than I had already shared.

Johnny took me to the malls and pampered me, buying me clothes and anything else that I needed. During this time, I ate my fill of fries. My cousins became a source of solace for me and, even though my ordeal left me without any meaningful expectations, spending time with them sparked a new awakening inside me. As the months passed, life began to return to my body, and I dared to play again during the day, jumping rope with my cousins in the garden. But, as soon as it was dark or I was alone, I sank with the sunset into sadness, disconnection, and feelings of being hopelessly lost.

14

Home

$\mathcal{I}$n December 1994, I boarded an airplane with my uncle, my aunt, and my cousins, and flew back to Kampala. From there, we took a bus to Kigali. Returning home was one of the things I had dreamt of and that marked a shimmer of hope in my darkened soul. I could not wait to meet and play with all my friends.

But the excitement was short-lived. After a month, I was back at school, staring the loss I had encountered all those months ago in the face again. The thought of returning to school immediately brought back memories of my mother. She was passionate about our education, and delighted in enticing my siblings and I to love school. I remembered how she would follow up on our studies every day when we returned home.

It made no sense for me to return to school without her encouragement spurring me on.

"What am I going to school for?" I asked myself. "Who will I show my report card to at the end of the term?"

In 1995, I stepped inside my new class, looked around, recognized nobody, and began the process of coping with normal life.

In retrospect, thank God, I was blessed to have survived with my father who pushed and guided me throughout my education.

Gallery

Uncle Huss Mugwaneza and his wife Annie Mugwaneza, died on April 7, 1994

Paternal grandfather, Eustache Kajuga, died on April 7, 1994

Uncle Maharangari, his wife Flora, and their five children—
Gilbert, Norbert, Mugeni, Liliose, and Clarisse, died on April 9,
1994

Mother, Norah Mukeshimana, Sisters Kayitesi Claudette & Francine Ingabire, Brother Claude Murengezi, died on April 10, 1994

Aunt Antoinette Kamisheke, her husband Kurujyishuri Joel, and their seven children, Victoire-Aimee Umuhoza, Clementine Girumuhoza, Felix Ntitetereza, Ferdinand Mwizerwa, Christine Uwase, Clement Ndayishimiye and Yvette Uwizeye, died in April 1994

Aunt Françoise, her husband Kayumba and their three children
—Lise, Dimitri, and Manzi, died in April 1994

Maternal Grandparents, Ruvuzumutego Leonidas and Joyce
Kankindi, died on June 24, 1994

Part III

15

Back To Life

*A*lthough I did not realize it at the time, reliving the Genocide moment by moment, often crying through the trauma of it all and allowing myself to feel the pain, was profoundly therapeutic and it was the true beginning of my journey towards healing. It took me two months of walking down the dark alleys of my memories to document everything I experienced, as I remembered it. It was extremely difficult and I had constant nightmares. I would wake up in the middle of the night and cry until morning. My heart was always heavy and sorrowful throughout the process. At the time, I could never have imagined that the handwritten entries in my journal would be the fuel that would ignite the fire in me to write this book.

I returned to school in 1995. There were no familiar faces in my new class, but I quickly made friends. On some level, our shared experiences connected us. Some of us had experienced the horrors of the Genocide, while others had come from neighboring countries where their parents had lived as refugees for over thirty years, leaving behind their friends and the life they knew to live in an unfamiliar country. Our individual experiences were so confusing and so horrific that we never spoke about them. Instead, we locked them up in boxes and slid them under our beds, deep into a dark corner where no beam of light could reach them.

In spite of it all, life went on, and I thank God for giving me the strength to pursue my studies. But, it always felt as if there were two different personalities dwelling inside me—one was lost, stuck, bitter, and completely disconnected from the present, while the other coped with life, obeyed the elders, and always put on a joyful face; her funny, bubbly personality barricaded the entrance to the dark recesses of her soul. I attended every social event to which I was invited. I was friendly with my classmates and the people around me. I performed well in school. I did what I was asked to do. I was not perfect, but I was always kind and courteous to the people around me. But I was broken inside. My soul refused to move forward. My inner self was in a cage, stuck in 1994.

When I passed my Primary Leaving Examinations (PLE) with outstanding results, I was the only one who was not celebrating. I did not feel the same joy that the people around me felt. For me, it was simply time to move onto the next chapter of my life—high school.

La Colombiere High School was an entirely different world and experience for me. The school was full of children from different countries, who told interesting stories in a sophisticated type of French that I had heard before. Kayitesi, who was gifted in learning languages, especially French, used to give me her books to read, and I quietly thanked her for giving me the opportunity to seamlessly blend into this new life in which I found myself.

As I grew into a teenager, so too did my love for music. I began to notice the handsome boys, and I had a crew of friends that I belonged to and with whom I partied. I had subconsciously developed a desire to make people happy. If getting good marks in school made my father happy, then I would work hard to achieve them for *him*. During therapy, I came to learn that this was a coping mechanism—one that I had quickly mastered. I had quite unintentionally, developed the appearance of a strong, fun, and easy-going girl, creating a suitable façade that kept me away from the hurt and broken person I was inside. I always felt like a fraud, struggling between these two different versions of myself.

Detachment

*W*hen I was home alone, in my room, with no opportunity to volunteer my time or organize an event, reality would creep in. The ten-year-old me would catch up and attempt to make up for lost time, but I never entertained her. She was no fun—all she had to share with me was a bag full of sorrow and trauma, and I wasn't ready to look inside. To avoid her, I would spend as little time with myself as possible. I was always on the lookout for the next social gathering and never hesitated to attend one when the opportunity arose. When there was no opportunity, I took the initiative and created one. I became skilled at organizing parties—wherever I was, there had to be a party with loud music playing. At home, I binged on watching movies to keep my mind occupied.

During commemorations of the Genocide against the Tutsis, we organized gatherings to commemorate my direct and extended family. Whether subconsciously or not, I refused to allow myself to revisit the memories and acknowledge the pain that came with them. Although I was physically present, I was emotionally detached. I avoided mourning my family, participating instead for the others who were hurting. I went out of my way to stand with them during their moments of grief.

A Spark Of Curiosity

*A*fter receiving my high school diploma in Business and Accounting, I enrolled at Université Libre de Kigali (ULK), with a dream of doing humanitarian work in a refugee camp or working with people who were hurting. Having been a refugee left me with a thirst that I believed could only be quenched when I helped others in similar situations. I opted to pursue a degree in Law, aiming to specialize in Humanitarian Law and work in places like Sudan.

Having not specialized in any form of Law during my high school years, I found the first few weeks of university quite difficult. Most of my classmates were familiar with the subject. I didn't understand their legal jargon, but I knew I was exactly where I was supposed to be. By the end of my first year, I had made many new friends. I had also established myself as somebody who could be counted on to arrange class study meetings, birthday parties, and social gatherings—anything that would keep me busy.

In the second year of my studies, my father encouraged me to apply for an internship. It was his strategy to shift my focus towards something more valuable to my life and my future. I was awarded a position at an enterprise called Sakirwa, which employed over three hundred people. Their human resources manager had recently resigned from her duties, leaving behind a huge pile of unfiled documents. My boss put me straight to work, instructing me to organize the documents according to their date of issue.

The work sparked a sense of curiosity in me that ignited a spark of excitement over finding something new to keep my mind busy. As I became more familiar with my job, I began setting time aside to take a closer look at the documents that passed through my hands. They were filled with rows of employees' names; each one assigned a figure calculated in Rwandan Francs.

"What are all these lists of names and figures I've been filing?" I asked my boss, Faustin.

"Those are lists of the company's payroll," he explained to me. "The employees' salaries."

I asked him about the calculations that led to the final figure on each document. Sensing my curiosity and interest, he began teaching me about taxes and everything that went into salary allocation, including how to calculate the figures on a computer. While he trained me, he would remind me of how smart I was, praising my work despite the fair share of mistakes I made. I felt validated. I thoroughly enjoyed the learning process and caught on to new concepts quickly. I realized there was a whole science behind the allocation of payroll; figuring out formulas and calculating salaries was fascinating to me. At the end of my three month internship, I asked my boss if I could apply for an extension. Instead, he opted to give me a position as the company's HR assistant—which is how I landed my first job.

Studying part time and working full-time meant that my time for partying was significantly reduced, something that I believe made my father happy. Although I was the HR Assistant, the company was in need of an HR Manager. Most of the responsibilities fell onto me, but I had limited experience. My great love for people opened up opportunities for me to interact with my fellow employees, something that my boss took note of and valued. Although I was only twenty years old at the time, observing how freely people confided in me, how they looked to me for help and counsel, and how I was readily available to receive them and to do what I could for them, he promoted me to HR Officer in Charge of Employee Relations. I enjoyed being part of their employee development programs and learning and growing in the field of human resources.

18

Gilbert

I met my husband, Gilbert, in 2005 through a friend. I was still in university, and he was living in Canada. My friend, who also lived in Canada, called me up one day and said "I have a cousin flying to Kigali soon, and I'd like you to show him around. He hasn't been there in ten years." I still believe to this day that her primary intention was to connect us.

Gilbert entered my life when I was in party mode. I took him out and showed him around the hottest spots and nightclubs in town. My friends and I would be partying, but he preferred spending time talking to me, asking me questions about my life and my family. "What's this guy's deal?", I often found myself wondering. Although I suspected the party scene was not his kind of lifestyle, he joined me no matter where I took him, making my friends and I laugh with his quirky sense of humor, but I always wondered why he had little interest in the joyful, giving side of me that I exposed so willingly.

One afternoon, over lunch, he ambushed me with an interesting observation. He hesitated at first, stumbling over his words, until he finally told me that in the three months that we had spent together, he could see that two different people were living inside me. Nobody had ever said anything like that to me. I had shared tiny pieces of my story with the people I cared about, but I limited what I told people about my survival of the Genocide to a general, superficial version of events— such as how, as a family, we had sought refuge with the nuns, but when the adults and older children were killed, our place of refuge became an orphanage; or how we walked from Kabgayi camp to Ruhango camp on foot.

"What do you mean?" I asked him. Although I was taken back by his question, I knew exactly what he meant.

"I feel as if there is a whole other part of you that we don't get to see."

Gilbert *saw* me, and seemed genuinely interested in getting to know this other person who was hidden inside me. To this day, I still wonder how he saw through me. Everybody else, and especially my friends, thought that I was simply a happy-go-lucky girl who enjoyed having fun.

Although he wanted to get to know this other person I carried inside me, it was time for him to return to Canada.

Unbeknown to me, the tightly closed door to my heart had been unlocked, and Gilbert and I stayed in contact. Over time, I slowly started opening up to him, sharing parts of my life with him that I had never shared with anyone else. I could not understand why it was so easy for me to share these intimate details with somebody that I had only just met. He became the first person to whom I gave the full, raw and uncut version of my 1994 ordeal. I did not speak about my feelings pertaining to what I had experienced, but, in general, I told him the details of the story. I would find myself sharing a memory, and he would gently probe me to continue telling how the events unfolded. Through his questions and my responses, he was able to see and understand me more clearly.

I recall complaining to him over the phone about a situation at home one day. After he was satisfied that I had finished my rant, he boldly suggested that I should consider seeing a therapist so that I could learn to let Mum go and accept what happened. "It looks like you are living your life like your mother's still alive, yet she's not," he said, adding, "This may come off as harsh, and I know that it's hard, but you need to grieve for your Mum and accept that she has left this world." This was the last thing I wanted to hear from anyone, least of all Gilbert, and I was deeply offended. Although it was the truth, it was disturbing to hear. I ended the call and decided not to talk to him again.

"Experiencing trauma as a child can lead to a host of emotional and psychological issues that may not emerge until later in life. Adults who experienced trauma during childhood may experience difficulties in many aspects of their lives. They may not realize that these traumatic experiences are contributing factors to their current issues or even the root cause of them." **Foundations Recovery Network** ("Problems Facing Adults who struggled with Trauma as a Child"- *Publication*)

19

Finding Love

*N*ot only did Gilbert and I speak again, but our relationship flourished. He was offered a good position in Rwanda, and, much to my delight, he returned home for good. Although I suspect that my presence may have influenced his decision to leave Canada, he would probably deny it.

Gilbert became my best friend. As we grew closer, he was not afraid to confront the truth in all its rawness and to ask the right questions—always with empathy. I had never been able to open up to another human being like I opened up to him—nobody had ever been able to get as close to me as he did. While I thought I was ugly inside, he was genuinely interested in and concerned with the part of me that was hurting. It was his selfless compassion that made me fall in love with him and say, "Yes," when he proposed to me in 2013.

Our relationship was often affected by my emotional instability. I subconsciously saw him as the person who would heal the wounds in my heart. I became unreasonably demanding of his time and energy, ambushing him with a barrage of demands at every turn, expecting him not only to have a finger on the pulse of my mood, but also to be able to provide a quick-fix solution for whatever was troubling me.

During the quiet times when I was alone, and I felt my spirit sinking and a dark cloud moving in, I would reach out to him. When he was unable to respond to me or get to me as quickly as I wanted him to, I would find myself withdrawing from him emotionally. "See you in a week," I would sometimes blurt out in frustration. But his patience was interminable. He would visit me after work and find me incensed and moody, but he would still hang around.

After we married, there were times where he was overwhelmed with work commitments, or he would arrive home too exhausted to have a cheerful time with me, and I would irrationally believe that there was something wrong with me—that I was a bad wife, and that I was not good enough for him. Feeling rejected by him, I would berate myself. I became desperate and clingy, and unconsciously expected him to fill the void left in my soul by the loss of my family—to say and do the things that they would have said and done.

I placed an enormous burden on Gilbert. He loved me, but my unfair expectations of him to be my constant refuge began to weigh heavily on him.

20

Professional Growth

*D*uring the remainder of my three years at Sakirwa, I completed my Law degree, and it was not long before I was promoted to HR Manager. Looking back, I had achieved so much in my young life and in such a short span of time. It was not until many years later that I realized that most of my achievements in school and the workplace were related to a need that lay deep within me to be involved in the development of people, both professionally and personally. I recognized that as I listened to the challenges of others, the more I was able to help people, the more validated I felt. When I gave my time to others, I felt normal and my soul felt a little lighter.

After graduating in 2007, I accepted an offer to join one of Rwanda's leading banks, the I&M Bank (the former Commercial Bank of Rwanda —BCR) as their new Employee Relations Human Resource Officer. The training and knowledge I gained during my three years with Sakirwa had fully prepared for me for this great opportunity. BCR was also where my father had once worked, and I was extremely excited, despite some underlying concern over my weak command of the English language.

Although I fit in well, I neither spoke nor wrote the language as well as my colleagues and English was the main language used by the bank. I knew that I had to master the language if I was going to have success there, and I embraced the challenge.

Fortunately, I was blessed with the support of my colleagues, especially Denise Umunyana. During my first week at BCR, I was required to send an email to the bank's three hundred and fifty employees, informing them of an event that the human resources department was organizing. Denise encouraged me to write what I could and then send it to her for editing. That email eventually made its way to every inbox in the bank's employee address book. I faced my fears and overcame my nagging doubts over being able to write in English to hundreds of people whom I considered to be far smarter than I was.

After that day, whenever I hesitated, thinking, "I can't do it," Denise would downplay my fears and tell me, "You *can* do it!". She pushed me beyond my limits and guided me to try different techniques to improve my writing. I gained a new sister in her and today we are business partners. I will always be grateful to her for her validation and guidance, and, most of all, her fearless attitude, which truly inspired me.

21

Back Pain

I suffered from occasional minor back problems since my high school days, but they were never severe enough to warrant worrying over. However, in 2010, my lower back became tense and it was excruciatingly painful. I struggled to get out of bed in the mornings, and I was eventually unable to stand up straight. I began walking with a terrible limp, and painkillers were ineffective. After a month of the symptoms showing no sign of subsiding, I visited the hospital. The doctors suspected a displaced disk and recommended surgery to correct it. My family was concerned about me being operated on at what they thought was a young age for a surgery. I returned to the hospital and opted to wear a back brace instead.

After spending two months in bed with no improvement, my doctor suggested that I start swimming. I had not swum regularly in over a decade. It reminded me of the joyous times I spent with my family and friends before the Genocide. Although it was fun back then, it meant little to me now. Getting back into swimming regularly meant opening that festering wound in my heart that I was so desperately trying to clamp closed. But if I was to avoid surgery and return to work, I had no other choice.

Fearful of losing my job, I decided to follow my doctor's recommendations. Within two weeks, the pain reduced somewhat, and I was able to return to work. I continued swimming every morning before going to the office.

During my healing journey, I discovered that my back pain was a symptom of the stress and trauma I was harboring from the Genocide —when unresolved emotions are not expressed, they find a way of manifesting themselves physically in the form of headaches, stomach pains and, in my case, backaches—which I still experience when I don't swim regularly.

22

Tikun Halev At Agahozo – Shalom Youth Village

*W*hile working at BCR, that old sense of purpose and the need to work in an organization that focused on helping people with deep needs, in addition to financial growth, began resurfacing in me. I knew that I was meant to be part of something much greater than where I was at the time.

After praying daily, an opportunity that changed the course of my life presented itself. Opening my inbox, I came across an e-mail from Anne Heyman, the founder of Agahozo- Shalom Youth Village. She was looking for an HR Manager for her organization, and a friend of mine had forwarded her my CV. Her email was an invitation to attend an interview in Rwamagana district, which is about fifty-five kilometers east of Kigali.

After thoroughly researching the organization, I was thrilled to discover that it focused on empowering orphaned and vulnerable Rwandan youth—mainly Genocide survivors—through healing, education, and love. Their emphasis on working with broken children touched my heart, and I immediately fell in love with their mission.

They were taking care of five hundred children each year from all thirty districts of Rwanda. They focused on all aspects of the child's health, with each incoming student receiving a medical and psychosocial assessment. They then received a treatment plan designed according to their specific needs before they were enrolled in ordinary high school classes.

In addition to high school education, the school provided each child with career guidance, counseling, and therapy. The after-school activities gave the children an opportunity to learn visual and instrumental arts, participate in team sports, and enrich their learning and personal development through entrepreneurship training and science centers.

What the organization was doing could not speak any clearer to my heart. I could hardly believe that something like this existed in Rwanda. There was no way that the ten-year-old me could resist this—it was exactly what I had been looking for, and my prayers had been answered.

During the interview, I enquired as to where I would find their offices in Kigali City, only to be told that I would be working in Rwamagana. My job downtown at the bank was only a five-minute drive from my home in Kimihurura, but this new position would mean a two-hour daily commute—one hour in the morning, and another in the evening.

Suddenly I was faced with a dilemma that I was not quite prepared for: with classes starting at 7:30 a.m., I would have to commute to and from work on the organization's bus with the teachers and the other administrative staff—and the bus hit the road at 6:00 a.m. I was also concerned about the new dress code, moving from corporate suits to jeans and sneakers. Joining Agahozo -Shalom Youth Village meant that I had to give up my morning swimming routine and make up for it on the weekends. There was a great price to pay for my prayers being answered.

With an intense inner battle raging, I sought counsel from my family and friends. Many of them found it difficult to buy into the idea of me quitting my current job and pursuing a career at a place that was not yet popular (at that time).

"What? Rwamagana? Don't go. You have a good job, a good car, and good friends," was the typical response.

Indeed, life as a BCR employee was fabulous. It was one of the best banks around. It employed a large number of young professionals and was a fun environment in which to work.

"And you are going *where*? Are you crazy, or what?" was another response. At that time, Agahozo - Shalom Youth Village was practically unheard of.

People's responses made sense, and I found myself doubting whether the opportunity was really for me. But my soul and the little girl that dwelled inside my heart felt otherwise—I could feel myself being gently tugged towards Rwamagana.

I was given three days to make a decision, but I asked for a week instead. At the end of that week, I decided to follow my heart, despite what everybody else was saying, and I felt completely at peace with my decision. I accepted the offer, signed the employment contract, resigned from the bank, and began my new journey at the youth village in November 2011.

My first two years there were somewhat technical, with most of my time and energy being spent setting up the Human Resources department. Coming from an environment where I was an HR Officer to setting up a whole department, there was much to be done. As the director of this department, I set up processes, created policies, and spent a great deal of time researching this new territory.

In 2014, I got involved in the children's programs. I attended workshops on working with children with troubled backgrounds, many of whom suffered from Post-Traumatic Stress Disorder (PTSD) and other conditions brought on by trauma. There was a Health and Wellness Center under which there was a program dedicated to providing psychological support. There was a Parental Wholeness program that gathered children with different cultures from all thirty districts and combined them into groups of sixteen under the same roof to teach them to live together in harmony.

With the continuous training around the Jewish value of *tikkun halev*—which means repairing the heart—I began to discover myself. I was deeply interested in the way the training focus was on getting to know a person on a deeper level. Rather than working solely on addressing intellectual needs, the programs ensured that these children envisaged a hope-filled future full of dreams, and a reason to live. Because the programs merged personal development with counseling and other support, the orphans were constantly given opportunities to develop critical thinking patterns and to heal from their wounds.

The trainers would ask crucial questions, and the inner me would be intrigued and want to respond to them. What I was learning was deeply personal. There were questions such as, "What does being successful really mean? Is it about getting to the highest level of your career, or is it about enjoying what you do, and having dreams?", or "What would be the indicators that our youth programs are having a positive impact?"

Anne Heyman, the founder of the youth village, had a mantra that went like this: "It's not a matter of how much you can do, but how invested your soul is. What is it that you see for yourself and your community, through it all?" The questions asked during management training were challenging, and I spent most of my two-hour commutes in deep contemplation about who I was, and whether or not I was truly connected to everything that was happening around me.

This was my first step towards hearing what the child within me really had to say. While learning to help others, I was helping myself, and I began to experience a profound shift within my soul. I took a leap of faith and finally started to give Celine a platform to meet and explore her inner child. I stopped running from myself, towards success, and took a step back to meet the young girl inside who was sad, hurt, and broken.

23

Fatigue

*I*n February 2015, I received the heart-shattering news that my father had fallen into a deep coma after suffering complications associated with hypertension and diabetes. After rushing to King Faisal Hospital and seeing him lying there in his bed, motionless, and in a critical condition, we wondered whether or not he was going to make it. I switched to "Action Mode"—my default setting in this kind of situation. My brain, numb to emotion, asked, "What can I do to regulate this situation? What do we do? What do we need? Who will spend the nights with him? Who will spend the days with him?" With my feelings locked away, I was able to cope.

Nobody expected him to recover, least of all me, but within two weeks of falling into the coma, he was discharged from the hospital. Those two weeks were a critical part of my healing journey. I like to believe that he died and was resurrected. He was diagnosed with diabetes, high blood pressure, and kidney failure, but, with the correct medication, he was able to manage his health as an outpatient.

With Dad safely back home, I returned to work, but I was so mentally fatigued that I felt like a zombie. My vision was blurry and an e-mail that would take usually half an hour to complete would take as long as a week. Work was becoming monotonous. I started developing slight aches at the back of my head that grew increasingly frequent and very painful.

I didn't know it at the time, but the stress over almost losing my father was causing my unresolved grief and trauma to resurface.

"What Makes People Remember a Traumatic Event after Such a Long Delay? At the time of a traumatic event, the mind makes many associations with the feelings, sights, sounds, smells, taste and touch connected with the trauma. Later, similar sensations may trigger a memory of the event. While some people first remember past traumatic events during therapy, most people begin having traumatic memories outside therapy. A variety of experiences can trigger the recall".

International Society for traumatic stress studies. ("Recovered Memories of Childhood Trauma"-Abstract from "Childhood Trauma Remembered." - *A Report on the Current Scientific Knowledge Base and its Applications* Research done by Susan Roth PHD & Matthew J. Friedman MD&PHD)

24

Isolation

*I*n April 2015, I attended a commemoration ceremony during which one of the survivors I had spent time with at the orphanage shared a testimony that took me back to that dark period—how our parents, siblings, and friends were killed, and how devastatingly confusing and hopeless it felt for us as children. The emotions that had overwhelmed me back then sprang back to life as I relived each moment in the present. I felt the tears welling up in my eyes and flooding down my cheeks, marking another step in my healing journey.

Accompanying my constant headaches, other signs of what was going on internally began to surface. I lost interest in parties and other events that I would have gladly attended or organized. Turning down one invitation after another, I started isolating myself because I no longer wanted to be around people. Not responding to phone calls became the norm. I lost my appetite and, by August 2015, I was completely out of touch with the rest of the world. I had no idea what I wanted to do or how I wanted to spend my time. Nothing stirred any sense of excitement in me. I lost touch with the world around me.

My friends were concerned and would always try to get through to me and help, by inviting me out for dinner, or to attend social gatherings. Gilbert was concerned too, although he assumed that I was overwhelmed with work and just too exhausted to do anything else.

25

The Voices

*I*t was impossible to focus for long periods of time at the office. Hours would pass with me sitting, my eyes fixated on the blank wall in front of me, my mind blank, tears trickling down my cheeks. I could not understand how it was possible to be crying uncontrollably without a provocative thought or hurtful event having spurred it. It was strange and confusing.

In September 2015, the voices started. The inside of my head was like a computer with countless folders and windows opening at the same time, performing multiple tasks like playing music, shuffling through documents, downloading apps, rendering and buffering high-quality HD videos and 3D graphics and animations. They were so many voices, all speaking simultaneously and loudly.

I told nobody of the voices. They became increasingly louder. There were times when I would sit in my office, holding my head tightly in my hands, silently screaming, "STOP! PLEASE STOP!"

One night, the voices had become so deafening that I was unable to sleep. I checked to see if Gilbert was asleep before creeping in the dark to the living room where I buried my face deep into a cushion and screamed my lungs out.

"STOP!" I screamed, but the voices remained.

Countless more sleepless nights followed. Sometimes, a week would go by without a wink of sleep, despite busy and exhausting days at work. I began to resent my job.

Gilbert realized that there was something seriously wrong with me, but when he asked me if I was okay, I would respond with, "I'm fine. I just need some rest."

Working at a school meant that we would share our vacation time with the children. This rest period helped me physically, but no matter how long the vacation period lasted, I remained mentally exhausted. We were off for the whole month of August, and I was certain that I would be sufficiently rested to be well by the time school started again in September.

Two weeks later, without any proper sleep, my body started to react. I walked on rubbery legs. When I did manage to fall asleep, I would wake up in a pool of sweat from nightmares filled with images of the dogs I saw eating corpses during the Genocide. One of the dogs was walking down the street with a human hand in its mouth. The nightmares would always end with me running for my life.

I began to resent life and had no desire to continue living. When I had the strength to speak over the voices, I would ask myself what was wrong with me, insisting that I pick up the broken pieces and pull myself together. I would attempt to rationalize, reminding myself that I had a great husband and a successful career—that unlike many others who survived the Genocide, I *had* a family.

But I did not want to live, not if it meant living like that.

Instead of spending the nights in bed with my husband, I paced the living room, Mumbling things that made no sense to me. I was losing my mind and my grip on reality, I was terrified.

Out of desperation, I approached Gilbert. "I don't know what's happening to me," I told him. "I may appear fine, but I'm far from it."

It was around 10.00 p.m., but Gilbert suggested that we go and see my aunt, Mama Lily, who was a nurse. Knowing that she was accustomed to dealing with all sorts of patients, we agreed that she would be the best person to advise us on what steps to take. For forty minutes, we drove from Kanombe to Nyamirambo. Having called ahead, she was waiting to meet us. While Gilbert waited for me in the living room, Mama Lily warmly and gently led me into her bedroom where we sat and talked. She listened closely and attentively as I told her everything I was going through, explaining all the symptoms I was experiencing, and how I felt exhausted, lost and confused.

She looked at me deeply for a moment, her eyes full of compassion. Mama Lily breathed in slowly and deliberately. "It is about time you got help," she said.

I didn't see that coming.

"What do you mean, '*got help?*' I asked, "And how?"

"Celine" she smiled warmly, "You have been through so much. I think you need to see a psychologist."

"Okay," I thought. I understood what a psychologist was. I had learned about psychology at Agahozo- Shalom Youth Village. But still, I couldn't wrap my head around what she meant when she said that I needed help. As far as I was concerned, I was suffering from exhaustion and I thought that I had perhaps contracted cerebral malaria.

After making multiple telephone calls, she said, "Tomorrow, I'm taking you to see a doctor in Ndera, but don't worry." Ndera is a village situated about fifteen kilometers away from Kigali and is well known for harboring Rwanda's most famous neuropsychiatric hospital, Caraes, widely and wrongly perceived as a place to which "crazy" people are taken. Being in the condition I was in at that moment, I offered no form of resistance and simply accepted the fact that I needed help. Wherever help was available, I was ready to be taken.

The next morning, we drove to Ndera. I was introduced to the lady who would be the first of several doctors I would meet during my healing journey.

She was a nun.

We sat down for our first session.

"How are you doing?" she asked.

"I am not well. I don't feel right."

She nodded. "Before we start working together, I would first like to get to know you better."

At that point, I had started crying. The more she said and the more she asked, the more I cried. The mere warmth and gentleness of her voice unlocked something inside me, and tears became a large part of my life from that point onwards. I cried as I ate my food. I cried as I sat in silence. It seemed like my tears had developed a mind of their own—I was unable to control them.

"I'd like to know all about you, the family you come from, how many siblings you have…" she said, giving me a blank piece of paper. "Please draw me your family tree. Whoever you can think of, just write them down, whether they are alive or deceased. After that, we'll take some time and talk about each of your family members and get to know more about them."

"I don't know how to draw," I said, feeling useless. "How do I do this?"

"That's completely fine", she replied graciously, "Whatever you can do is perfect, even if you just use dots."

She asked me if I preferred plain or colored pencils. I immediately fell in love with her approach of using art and creativity, making the experience colorful—and even fun. She seemed genuinely interested in understanding me and the wounds I carried.

I put pencil to paper and started drawing. As we made progress, she handed me two colored pencils. "Use the green one to mark your family members that are still alive," she gently instructed me, "and the red one to mark the deceased ones." She turned on the radio and helped me as I went through my family tree from my grandparents to parents, uncles and aunties, their siblings, their children, my siblings and cousins, and anybody else she could help me think of. As I did what she asked me to do, I realized that about seventy percent of my family members were marked in red. Seeing my family tree so full of red crosses brought me to tears, and I wept uncontrollably for the remainder of the session.

"You are going through a crisis," she said gently once the tears had subsided, "But I'm not going to prescribe any medication for you just yet. I want to have a few more sessions with you first. Please come back in the next few days, and let's talk some more."

I was back in Ndera two days later for a more interactive session than the first one.

Returning to the family tree, we spoke about those whom I had named.

"Tell me about him," she asked, "And tell me about her," and I would tell her everything I could remember through floods of tears. We spoke about the deceased family of my uncle, his wife, and their five children, my grandparents, and my cousin Vicky's family of nine.

She asked about my siblings, Lyrette and Michael, who were born when my father remarried after the Genocide, and she got a more positive reaction from me—my half-brother and sister were one of the few things that brought joy to my heart after everything I had been through. She tackled every area of my life from all directions, trying to understand me deeply and fully while balancing the negative and the positive aspects.

Eventually, *I* started asking questions.

"What's *wrong* with me?" I lamented, "What's going on? Why is this happening to me *now*, and out of nowhere?"

"Your soul has been chained and suffocated for a long time," she explained, "and I think it has grown weary. It's time for you to listen to the ten-year-old in you. It's time to connect with every single thing that you went through and experienced growing up, whether good, bad, or challenging. Your soul needs to confront each of these things accordingly."

I nodded, taking it all in. "Why do I feel unable to move forward? I feel blocked," I asked, the questions flooding my mind, desperate for answers. "Can I not just close the door and continue living? I've been doing it my whole life. Why can't I do it now?"

∾

"Early life adversity is a major risk factor for the development of psychological and behavioral problems later in life. Higher rates of depression, suicidality, anxiety disorders, post-traumatic stress disorder and addictions, have been reported in adults who experienced childhood traumatic events." **Australian Psychological Society.** ("How childhood trauma changes our hormones, and thus our mental health, into adulthood" _ *Study* by Femke Buisman-Pijlman, Senior Lecturer Addiction Studies, University of Adelaide)

26

Calling It Quits

*I*n the midst of therapy, work became increasingly overwhelming. I could barely type or send an e-mail. Seemingly insignificant matters irritated me. My anxiety levels were at an all-time high and being asked something as simple as, "What time are we having the meeting?" would see me breaking out in a cold sweat and lashing out in rage at an unsuspecting colleague. In the past, meeting requests and arrangements were a normal part of my working day, but now they felt like insurmountable tasks.

One day, it had me thinking, "I am the head of Human Resources, and I have a great responsibility. I am being paid a large sum of money to work, but I have not been doing it to the best of my abilities."

To be true to my employers and myself, I decided to quit. I asked my boss, Jean Claude Nkulikiyimfura, for an appointment outside of work. When we met, I got straight to the point.

"JC," as I called him, "I'm going through a difficult time. I still don't know exactly what is wrong with me, but I am seeing a therapist. I am being paid for work that I am not doing, and this is not fair to your organization. I would like to resign from my job."

His response surprised me.

"You have helped this organization for a while now," he smiled, "And you have accomplished so much. Now that you are sick, how about we take care of you instead?"

I stared at him in disbelief. "I would understand if you would still like to resign after your treatment and recovery," he continued, "But for now, I cannot accept your resignation. Take all the time you need, get well, let us help you, and we will proceed from there."

"I feel like I want to stop everything," I said, resisting his kindness, "I don't want to work at all."

But JC was not taking no for an answer. "You are such a great employee," he said warmly, "You are not doing us any wrong at all. Allow us to be there for you for a change. Why don't you go home and think about it?"

Despite his compassion, the spirit of integrity that my mother had instilled in me would not allow me to yield. I no longer had the same passion for my work, and it felt unfair to the organization to receive payment for work that somebody else would now be paid to do.

"How about I work part-time, and you cut my salary in half?" I suggested.

"We don't have to reduce your pay," he replied quickly.

I firmly stood my ground, "I will not allow that, JC," I insisted, "Personally, I feel as if I have only been working part-time, so why should I be paid a full-time salary?"

He finally gave in, and we agreed to draw up a new contract. I was to work part-time, two days a week. This new arrangement was such a relief to me. As I signed the document, the pressure of feeling dishonest and unfair was lifted from my shoulders.

Beyond this, I felt truly validated—that my work was appreciated, and I was not a disappointment.

27

The Affirmation

While I was healing, my head ached constantly. It felt so heavy that I could barely hold it up straight. My back hurt so much that I started walking as if I was carrying a bag of cement on my shoulders, dragging my feet along the ground. It would take me ten minutes to walk from the staff bus to my office, a distance I once easily covered in two minutes. Determined not to have my problems be discovered by my boss and colleagues, I would pretend that I was busy on the phone, stopping every few steps to disguise the pain. Once inside my office, I would lock the door and crawl onto my desk, lying across it in agony. I thought I was dying.

I remember crying and praying to God, asking Him what was happening to me and why I was going through all this pain. On one particularly trying day, a clear, gentle, compassionate voice spoke to me in the midst of my quiet sobs. "My daughter," the voice said, "This is a journey you need to go on to heal—not just for you, but for your family, for your country and for the world. Your story is going to touch the hearts of many others and help them on *their* journeys." It told me to start writing things down, reminding me that "You are going to need it, going forward."

The voice I heard was the voice of God. I felt connected to Him in a way that I had never been connected before. Despite having my husband, my aunt and a wonderful therapist walking with me, I felt incredibly lonely inside, but that morning, despite the pain, I felt a higher spirit carrying me.

When I arrived home that evening, I took out my journal and began to write. Reflecting on my encounter with God that morning marked the end of my crisis and the beginning of my healing. There was a strong sense that I was, symbolically, leaving the emergency room and preparing to receive my medication as an outpatient. I was still in pain and terrified, but I slowly started to make peace with what I was going through, realizing that the more I resisted it, the deeper I would be affected by it. I had to make daily, difficult, and conscious decisions to embrace the reality that was my sickness/trauma and embark on my healing journey, one day at a time.

28

Tied To The Future - Right Seat Ltd

*B*ack in the day, while working in the HR department at the bank, Denise and our colleagues often spoke of leaving and opening an HR company together at some point in the future. In early 2015, Denise called us all together and we brainstormed how we could get the business off the ground. Although there was no shortage of enthusiasm, nothing ever materialized.

As the months passed by, thoughts of opening the business became all-consuming for Denise and I. I tossed and turned at night, knowing that it was now or never. It was not about the money, but rather an opportunity to create something new and impactful. By the end of May, I could no longer contain myself. I called Denise.

"You know what, Denise?" I said, getting straight to the point, "Let's start that company, even if the others aren't ready."

By 7:30 a.m. on the second of June, Right Seat Ltd was registered. This marked the beginning of an incredible entrepreneurial journey—another book in itself. It was an amazing and great opportunity that was anchoring me to the future. It was God's way of forcing me to plan for a life beyond today, a life of creating something new, while learning and serving the community.

In September 2015, we signed our first client—we were in business.

With the agreement to work part-time at Agahozo - Shalom Youth Village still firmly in place, I had the time to go to my therapy sessions, slowly grow the business, and had the freedom to work without feeling guilty if I was unable to focus on the business for any length of time. Denise joined the business on a full-time basis in January 2016, while I continued to juggle working at Agahozo - Shalom Youth Village twice a week.

Having Denise, my friend, mentor, role model, and soul sister as my business partner helped me to hold myself accountable as I tended to this new venture in my life. Like a newborn baby, it required nourishment and feeding. Having something important to take care of and to hold onto allowed me to pull myself forward at my own pace; it provided me with a sense of balance as I continued on my healing journey.

By June 2017, the business had grown exponentially and required my permanent involvement. I approached JC and told him that I was resigning with six months' notice. We drafted an exit strategy and a plan to find a suitable replacement. By January 2017, I was full time on board with the new business.

Part IV

29

The Fear Of Rejection

*M*y first therapist became increasingly unavailable, and I grew weary of the long gaps between sessions. I eventually sought out a new therapist who picked up from where I left off, digging deeper into my heart to unearth the sources of the issues I was dealing with.

We spent a great deal of time focusing on ten-year-old me. Our sessions were filled with conversations about how *she* really felt. We spoke about her fear when the soldiers invaded her home on the seventh of April, 1994. We explored the prayer she recited when her life was threatened.

I admitted that, not only had I felt rejected by my family, but also by Jesus Himself. When He pulled me back to Earth, He also pulled me away from my family. I felt cheated. I did not understand why He had done that to me.

We explored how I felt when my family was killed. We spoke about the *Interahamwe* and their death threats, and how I secretly held out a sense of hope each time there was a possibility that I, too would be killed. In my mind, death was a passage to a happier life. But death never came. Through therapy, I realized that I had felt rejected by death too.

Mum had always taught us to speak with integrity, but with Heaven rejecting me, I felt as if she had lied to me, that she did not honor our agreement and had broken her promise. Mum, together with my brother and sisters, pushed me away before they were killed. It was as if Mum had decided that I would live without asking what *I* wanted. But it was the right thing for them to do, even though, as a young child, having them leave like that made *no* sense to me. Even though pushing me away gave me a chance to live, I struggled to shake the feeling of rejection that cut deeply.

As I grew older, I believed that my family had sacrificed themselves for me, and, over time, guilt and shame invited themselves in. How dare I feel disappointed and hurt by them for leaving me when they had given up their lives so that I might live?

"I was prepared to die with them," the ten-year-old me would shout, stomping her feet into the ground, "I wasn't prepared to live without them."

I was angry at myself for the conflicting emotions I felt, torn between rejection and blame. I had no right to feel rejected, especially after what they had done for me. I should have felt a sense of immense gratitude towards them, but I did not and could not. The ten-year-old me and the present day were at war with each other.

Through the therapy sessions, we worked on resolving this inner conflict. I found myself justifying my Mum's and my siblings' decision, saying that I completely understood why they did what they did— because it made sense. I knew that if I were ever in my family's shoes, I would do the same for my children and siblings without a moment's hesitation. My therapist skillfully redirected me from what made sense to giving me space to acknowledge my feelings of frustrations, disappointment and hurt—something that was exceptionally difficult for me to do. It took a month of painful moments with tears, and another two months of further exploration, to slowly acknowledge everything the ten-year-old me was voicing, and then to actually *experience* those feelings.

Although my deep-seated fears of rejection and abandonment were confusing topics to explore, I learned to understand that what I was going through was perfectly normal, and acceptable. The more I shared my memories and feelings with my therapist, the more I felt the heavy weight of my experience relieved. With every sigh of relief, I felt calmer. When I was able to sleep again at night, I realized that the therapy was working.

30

The Fear Of Attachment

*D*espite being able to sleep again, as we uncovered new issues, the headaches persisted, and my back began to hurt again. Having not exercised for some time, my therapist suggested that I do so and I agreed to go swimming once a week. With God's voice still resounding in my mind, reminding me that "this is a journey I need to go on to heal," I remained accountable and stuck to my weekly exercise regimen, even when I didn't feel like it.

Something that emerged during my therapy sessions was how emotionally distant I was in my close personal relationships. I refused to become attached to anyone out of an irrational fear of them dying and leaving me. As hard as I tried, I could not shake the feeling that those I loved would be taken from me.

Through therapy, I discovered that I was going through life subconsciously waiting for my turn to die. It was only when I gave the ten-year-old me a voice that I realized how prepared and expectant she was for her life to be over. My therapist took me back in time to when I desperately hung on to Mum's *kitenge,* refusing to let go, determined to die with her. I had been living with that same determination since childhood, where dying and joining my family felt like the right thing for me. The only thing I truly looked forward to was death, and I felt guilty and ashamed for being ungrateful for everything I had achieved.

My life was not a matter of living, it was a matter of existing—going through the motions and moving from one day into the next. Despite my accomplishments, it was as if my soul was unable to keep up with the successful life I was living. The more milestones I reached, the heavier I felt, torn between the child who should have died and the adult who had not only survived, but who was thriving—externally. The more successful I was, the more I felt I was disconnecting from the person I was, losing a little piece of the old me, alienating myself from the little girl that I clung onto inside. While I was making strides on the outside, internally, I found myself regressing, unable to fully appreciate my successes—it was almost as if the successes were not my own. It always felt as if I was living a double life.

Regular therapy validated that, what I perceived to be abnormal and irrational feelings and behaviors were quite understandable, after a traumatic event. This realization was a difficult, piercing truth to face, but it liberated me. It took me three months to learn how to accept my reality, but when I did, it opened more doors to my healing. With another burden removed from my shoulders, I began to feel lighter inside.

31

Grieving

*H*aving confronted and made peace with my reality, a burning question remained:

"Now that I know what is wrong with me," I asked my therapist, "What is next? How do I dream big? How do I live in the moment and celebrate life?"

"The first step is to begin the proper grieving journey," she said, smiling gently, "This wound is part of your life story and, although it will leave a scar, it can be healed."

She told me that, by holding onto my deceased family, I was preventing myself from healing and moving forward. She suggested that once I had let my family go, the next step would be to work on reconciling the ten-year-old me with the thirty-year-old me.

"You'll need to introduce the younger you to the person you've become," she said.

Up until that moment, I had never made time to listen to the ten-year-old girl who was trapped deep inside me, looking for a way out. She was still huddled up there in the corner of my soul, alone in the dark, heavy-laden, hurting, weeping, and bitter. Because I firmly believed that nobody would love her and want to be associated with her in any way, I had chosen to completely ignore her. People seemed to enjoy and appreciate the livelier version of me—myself included. While in the company of others, I lived in a fairytale world with no issues, sadness, or pain of any kind, but the time had come to be jolted back to reality, to meet my inner child, and to listen to what she yearned to share. It was time to grieve.

Grieving was a subject that I barely understood, but with my therapist's help and some in-depth research, I came face to face with the enormity of the emotional task that lay ahead of me. Besides the last three days that I saw my family, from the seventh to the tenth of April 1994, I had shared little else of my family with my therapist. As we began the grieving process, she asked me to talk about each family member individually and share my favorite memories of them. I had never considered exploring such matters before.

She began by asking me about my mother, encouraging me to ask my father when there were things that I could not remember. Over time, interesting stories about my mother began to surface, and my interest in the kind of person she was grew. I developed a strong desire to know as much as possible, not only about Mum, but about my siblings as well —what they liked, and what their funniest stories and moments were.

During this time, I remembered a videotape my family had recorded in 1989 during a Christmas that we spent with our paternal grandparents. There were hours of footage of our large family, including my Mum and my siblings. Remembering this sparked an idea to ask my father and Johnny to sit with me and talk about our lost loved ones—something we had never done. Dad and Johnny loved the idea and agreed to record the conversation with the assistance of a counselor from a mental health awareness initiative, called Sana. For the first time in my life, I was able to talk about the tragic massacre of our family. After five hours of the three of us revisiting and sharing the memories of my Mum and my siblings—something that ended up being a family therapy session—a one-hour recording entitled "Our Family Story

#Kwibuka" was produced and subsequently shared with the world on YouTube.

Mum was the one who instilled the quality of independence in us. Whenever Mum and Dad traveled together and left us at home, she would say, "Learn how to do things on your own. Let the older ones help the younger ones. And remember, your dad and I will not always be with you." By the time I was ten years old, I had disciplined myself to tidy my room and wash my clothes three times a week.

Mum taught us to be hard workers and good students. She would not tolerate a child who did not study and obtain good grades. She bought us books and read Bible stories to us, making us recite the stories of Saul, David, Joseph, and others. She was serious about teaching us Godly values and Biblical principles—ill manners were inexcusable in her eyes. We were to be polite, honor our elders, love school, and culti-vate inner beauty. Lying was sacrilege—we were free to make mistakes, but we were not permitted to lie. We were expected to be people of integrity, even when nobody was watching. Although I never understood what she meant, I remember her repeating over and over again to my siblings, "Be people of integrity."

As I eagerly shared my discoveries with my therapist, I discovered how much power there was in telling these stories. Hearing myself giving voice to these precious memories helped me to integrate the past into the present. When there were no more vivid memories of Mum to recall, we went through one family member after another. Each happy memory painted a clear picture of everything I had lost, over and above their presence in my life. The process was incredibly painful, but it was necessary to acknowledge and grieve that which I had lost. It meant allowing every emotion I had buried deep inside me to surface so that I could freely express it—sadness, anger, loss, frustra-tion and helplessness, all rolled into one.

It also meant writing letters addressed to each of them, not only to share my grief over their deaths, but also to bring them up to speed in terms of my life as an adult, which included introducing them to my husband and sharing my many accomplishments, including that of my business. Because Mum was a businessperson when she was alive, I shared the most information about that part of my life with her. She was the first to know when I won a new client or when I received a check. Although she was not physically present to share in my successes and setbacks, it felt good to involve her in my present life:

Dear Mum,

Today, at the age of thirty-three, I look back and thank you for the values of humility, obedience and hard work you tirelessly taught me from a tender young age. When you told us, "One never knows—your dad and I are not always going to be around", it was as if you knew how soon you would depart.

Thank you for instilling the value of integrity in me. I often heard you reminding my sisters that cultivating beauty from within was more important than cultivating outer beauty. Thank you for teaching me to act with grace and to remain true to myself, no matter what. These values led me to where I am today.

I followed in your footsteps and opened a business. You will love Denise Umunyana, my business partner. She is a warrior just like you. I will tell you more about the business and our beautiful, new country in my next letter.

I'm married now. You would love Gilbert. In fact, when I think about it, I think that you and him would have teamed up against me had you been alive today. He is respectful and funny, and always finds a way to cheer me up.

Could you hug Kayitesi, Francine, and Claude for me? Please let them know that I am writing to them right after this. Send kisses to my two grandpas and grandma, and my uncles, aunties, and cousins.

I am encouraging the rest of the family here to write to everyone too.

Missing you so much,

Your daughter, Celine

32

Learning To Live Again

---

*I*t dawned on me one day that I was not the only member of my family who was dealing with trauma. Of the surviving members of my family, including my father and my brother, none of us had *ever* sat down and talked about what we went through in 1994—twenty years of silence lay buried inside each of us. I began to wonder whether Rwanda, as a country, had healed from its wounds. I wondered whether other Rwandans were going through the same grieving process that I was experiencing. Now that I was beginning to come to terms with my own trauma, I asked myself whether others like me had *really* allowed themselves to feel the pain of the Genocide and talk openly about their experiences.

Despite the annual commemoration ceremonies where survivors would cry briefly, for most people, the trauma was so deep that it was easier to block the pain, lock it away, and then simply *exist*—as I had done for so long. For most Genocide survivors, life had become a mechanical cycle of coping with the trauma, rebuilding our lives, and trying to make the most of what we had left

I thought about my brother, Johnny, and how close he had been to

Mum and my older siblings. For the first time, I wondered whether he had ever grieved their sudden and brutal deaths. Married, with four children of his own, he had been preoccupied for the greater part of his adult life. Perhaps, like me, he had locked his grief safely away, hoping it would never resurface.

While attending church one Sunday, I noticed an advertisement for an upcoming six-month counseling course playing on the big screen up front. I knew instantly that God was drawing my attention to the work He was calling me to do. By asking me to endure the healing process, the picture He had depicted for my life was unfolding right before my eyes: My personal story was going to be used as a tool to help someone else.

One day, I decided to share my story with Johnny for the first time. I visited him and took him through the healing journey I had been on for the past year. When I had finished speaking, he fell silent for a while before looking up at me. His eyes were brimming with tears. "We all need therapy," he said, "We all need a platform to grieve and heal. I commend you for having the courage to take this step—some of us are not as brave." The validation of his words erased any of my remaining insecurities, and further fueled me to pursue the counseling course.

Deep inside my soul, I knew that there was something more that God was calling me to do, but I could not yet see what it was. One night, while writing to Kayitesi, an idea came to me to go beyond simply journaling my memories in a notebook and to combine everything together in the form of a memoir.

Self-doubt immediately crept in, clouding my mind with questions: "Is it really necessary to put my story out there? Am I not just playing the victim and seeking unnecessary attention? Do I really want to continue revisiting these painful memories?" I found myself searching for reasons *not* to go through with it, conjuring up all sorts of excuses to validate my reservations: "Nobody is going to be interested in reading your book," the voices in my head would shout. "It will not help anyone. It will not be well written. Are you ready for negative feedback and bad reviews?"

As many excuses as there were not to write the book, there were countless reasons to go ahead. It felt right. It would be a massive leap from where I was, and I sensed that being vulnerable and openly sharing my story with the world could be the channel for another person's healing—even if it was just one person. This alone gave me a reason to live. The more confirmations I received, the more the excuses faded into the background. It might not be a perfect book but it will definitely make an impact. I could feel my courage growing, and I felt confident that I had the inner strength to persevere through whatever lay ahead and see this through to the end.

I thought about how many other Rwandan hearts were still heavy-laden, but, despite this, Rwandans are incredibly courageous. When I think about the country's development since 1994, and the impact that Rwanda is making around the world despite its tragic past, it is a reflection of the resilience and strength of every Rwandan. I knew that I would be doing both myself and my country a great disservice if I did not heed my calling.

I decided to stop my therapy sessions. With a new sense of calling, I signed up for the counseling classes and began the process of learning how to help others, and ourselves. With every class, I felt more alive. I made new friends who shared the same calling and interests as me and who, like me, saw the need to raise an awareness about healing and mental health. I learned about empathy and, as this new-found skill developed inside me, I started to see people differently—I developed an ear that heard the silent words that people chose not to share.

Although my therapy taught me to face my past and reconcile it with the present, it was through the counseling classes that I learned about my present-day relationships and the impact that my traumatic past was having on them. By avoiding the perceived pain associated with becoming attached to people, I had inadvertently created a storm of emotional instability inside me. My deeply entangled emotions made me moody and unpredictable. I learned that it was the unresolved trauma that was creating my inner turmoil, but I knew that there was a way out and that I could become a psychologically healthier person.

I began to understand why I lacked self-confidence growing up—having my mother, who was also my role model, and my sisters snatched away from me at such a young age left me with no familiar female role model to guide and validate me, or anyone to whom I could go to for emotional support. As I grew older, I found myself seeking approval in every area of my life, feeling inadequate when I was not recognized for a job well done—especially in my work environment. On the occasions when I *was* acknowledged, I self-destructively refused to believe that any of it was true.

Looking inward, I noticed a tendency to block painful or negative emotions. I observed how I would condemn myself when these feelings surfaced. My shame and guilt over having survived left me believing that I had no right to fuss or fret over any challenge I faced. I was supposed to be grateful for my life and everything I was blessed with—after all, I reasoned, there were other people out there who didn't even have a meal to get them through the day.

I suffered from erratic mood swings, but I did not realize how confusing this was to the people who were close to me, specifically Gilbert, Denise, and my other close friends, Josiane, Dora and Yasmine. I can only imagine how difficult it was for others to be around me, not knowing how to handle themselves in fear of setting me off. One moment, I would be happy and social, but suddenly quiet and moody the next.

While acknowledging my unhealthy emotional patterns, I took the time to journal, writing down my thoughts and feelings as they came to me. I meditated and prayed about them, discussing them with God as I tried to untangle them and determine their source, to learn to navigate them. Jesus was my wonderful counselor, just as it was promised in Isaiah 9:6. I realized that having emotions, even the negative ones, was perfectly natural and that forcing myself not to feel sad (or to experience any other negative feeling, for that matter) did nothing more but feed these emotions, allowing them to grow unattended in the dark recesses of my mind.

Through the counseling classes, a new light was shone on these dark areas of my psyche, giving me a place to validate, understand, and accept these feelings and where they were coming from. Refusing to speak about these emotions chewed me up inside, but releasing them in a healthy way helped me to deal with them appropriately.

33

Triggers

$\mathcal{T}$hese new revelations exposed the various triggers that set my emotions off—my horror when I discovered an error I made in an e-mail after sending it to a client, or how I reacted when Gilbert was emotionally unavailable. The feelings would, without fail, send me plummeting on a downward spiral of convincing myself that I was good for nothing.

Dealing with these triggers meant acknowledging them first—"Yes, I feel rejected."

This would be followed by taking some time to think about the source and creating a mechanism to safeguard my heart: "But is it really because I'm a bad person? Did I actually do anything wrong?"

It was important that I learned to navigate through my feelings in a healthy way. This often meant taking a deep breath and validating myself—just because I made a mistake, or my feelings were not acknowledged, did not mean that I was worthless.

The next step would be to determine how to correct the issue so that I could deal with it appropriately if the incident reoccurred itself in the future. This was usually where the practice of empathy came in—for example, in Gilbert's case, seeing things from his perspective and understanding that he might simply be having a bad day, or that business was perhaps not going well for him.

Being aware of my triggers is a form of self-care that I work on daily. I am now able to identify and deal with any negative emotions before they can escalate and spoil my mood for the rest of the day. Nobody else can do this work for me. By taking care of myself, I am putting myself first, loving myself unconditionally so that I can extend that love to others from deep within.

This newfound knowledge marked the beginning of the next phase of my healing journey. Healing from my past meant that I could no longer continue merely existing from one day to the next. It was time for me to *live*. My hopes for the future grew stronger every day. I was able to navigate my emotions in a healthy way when I was having a bad day. I was growing a new business, taking on new employees, clients, signing new and larger contracts—*and* I had found out my calling. Within two years of Right Seat Ltd having opened its doors, our list of clients and staff had increased fivefold, with thousands of applications having passed through our recruitment process since then. My new business had become my anchor, grounding me in the present and tying me to the future. My heart was open to receive the joy associated with my accomplishments. I found myself looking forward to each new tomorrow. For the first time, the future felt *tangible*. I was eager to write my book, even though I had no idea how or when it would happen.

34

Unlearning In Order To Learn

*D*espite making new discoveries and taking the necessary steps along my healing journey, one of the biggest challenges I faced was unlearning the behavior that was so deeply rooted in my system. Undoing certain practices, unbelieving ingrained beliefs, and rewiring my defense mechanisms meant evolving into a new version of myself— and evolution is rarely a comfortable process. I could no longer hide behind my mask because my true self had been unveiled and exposed—turning back was not an option.

Transitioning to this new version of myself was a little frightening and somewhat disconcerting. I wanted to heal, but healing meant allowing myself to *feel* the pleasure and the pain that life invoked. Doing this was foreign to me, but I had to learn. I had to analyze and understand how I functioned in, and reacted to, everyday situations. Letting go of the Celine I had been up until that point in my life required more inner strength than I ever could have imagined. I found myself asking questions like, "Who am I now?" and "How do I live my life now?"

As I learned not to overbook my schedule with unnecessary activities, I had to learn to become comfortable living in those moments of tranquility. Although the absence of the constant busyness that I had become accustomed to living with provided me with tremendous peace of mind, I often found myself itching to find something that needed to be done. But taking the time to realize and reassure myself that I had completed my tasks, allowed me to start appreciating these periods of rest without any feelings of guilt.

One day, the Holy Spirit visited me and made me realize that my relationship with God also needed to be restored. My relationship with God was not an intimate one. My trauma had created a disconnected and superficial relationship based solely on the few biblical principles I had learned at home as a young child. I was born into a Christian family, so I was accustomed to going to church on Sunday, reading a verse from scripture on Saturday, and saying my prayers before eating or during times of trouble. I carried these basic principles into my workplace, praying only when I had problems needing to be resolved.

Besides my daily prayers, my Sunday church service routine was the only measure of my faith. It was only when I started my healing journey that I poured my heart and soul out onto Jesus' feet. My quiet times brought me closer to Jesus, trusting Him to walk with me and to help me heal, despite the fear that came with not knowing who I was anymore. One thing I was certain of was that I no longer carried the ten-year-old Celine inside me—she was finally free to grow up, with a renewed sense of hope, purpose, and aspiration of one day helping others on their own healing journeys.

Being transparent with and trusting Him with my pain was a new experience for me. I had to open up to Him, both through prayer and through letters where I told Him how I had felt rejected by Him as a little girl, especially after I prayed to be in Heaven with my family— and how those prayers went unanswered. I asked Him why He had allowed the Genocide to take place, why so many people had to die such brutal, violent deaths, and where He was while it was happening. Being authentic with Him in this way helped me feel safe in His presence, knowing that I could ask the questions I needed to ask, no matter how difficult, without fear of condemnation. It was liberating to know that He could receive and handle all my rebellious questions with grace.

I knew of God's love—I had seen it through Christ's crucifixion—but I had never personally experienced it. I did not know or understand what it meant to be accepted by Him. Although I could feel the sadness being flushed from my heart, I still felt empty inside because I had not yet received His love.

Protecting myself from the possibility of my loved ones being taken from me again had done more damage than good. By blocking them out, I had plunged myself into a world of deep loneliness. By refusing to allow God or my community to sojourn with me, I missed out on the support system that I had all along.

As I moved forward with Him, day-by-day and step-by-step, I felt my soul being liberated. However, I realized that there was a significant amount of spiritual work that still needed to be done—work that could only be done by God, if I allowed Him to do so. I could hear him telling me, "When you get out of your cocoon and fully experience day-to-day life, that is when you will find Me waiting for you with My arms wide open. I cannot force you out of your protective shell—you have to be willing to step out of it all on your own."

These words formed the bridge I needed to finally meet Him.

Jesus Christ revealed to me that the Heaven I dreamed of—the Heaven represented by my family—was only complete when God Himself was present. This new revelation fortified my spiritual health—I was thirsty for God in an entirely new way, and I looked forward to meeting Him.

That day, the day I met God, those feelings of loneliness vanished into thin air like smoke. The sadness that had been eating me alive like a cancer disappeared.

I am not a born again Christian by name or because it was the right thing to do—I was born-again because I received His undying love for me and experienced what it meant to have Jesus as my personal savior. I saw that the whole purpose of Christ's crucifixion and the work He was doing in and through me—the work that had brought me so much healing—was so that I might have eternal life. The work I do during my time here on Earth would have no meaning if there were nothing more to it.

My journey towards healing allowed my soul to receive love, not only from God, but from other people as well. Through prayer and studying God's Word, I am still learning to grasp the meaning of His love in the greater scheme of things. I am still seeking to fully understand what it means to be referred to as *His daughter*.

By walking with God and allowing Him to guide me, He continuously reveals to me what a loving Father He is—just like it says in the Bible, His Word.

A New Beginning

*O*ne of the reasons for me being unable to celebrate any great moment, achievement or accomplishment was the fear of being disappointed or heartbroken if my expectations of everything being okay in the end did not materialize. I anticipated mishaps at every turn. I did not expect anything good to last. I believed that the day would eventually come when it would all be taken away from me.

I realized that, as human beings, many of us carry a fear of hope. I know I most certainly did. I was afraid to hope at all.

I was fearful of messing up and losing a new job even before I started it. Instead of celebrating the signing of a new contract or the acquisition of a new client, any possible joy would be drowned out by the alarm bells that would be clanging loudly in my mind, reminding me not to be too hopeful or become too comfortable. There was always that voice whispering in my ear, reminding me that I should not expect to ride the wave of success for too long because it wouldn't last.

There was little inner joy to be found while traveling abroad, visiting friends and family, or during our couple's quiet time at home, comfortable in our pajamas on movie nights. I would find myself preparing to lose Gilbert or my friends and family at any time. Rather than enjoying a moment for what it was, I would allow the negative thoughts that perpetuated my fear of losing them to destroy everything.

Life is unpredictable, and we cannot always control what comes our way, but I have learned how important it is to acknowledge, embrace, and celebrate the beautiful moments when they are gifted to me, and always with gratitude towards God. Tasting the crisp, fresh air that accompanies each new achievement and stopping to savor the taste of each celebratory ice cream has made me realize how much I had been missing out on before. Today, the simple joys of being alive, like waking up in the morning and enjoying a wholesome, nutritious breakfast, or spending time visiting a friend, are not overlooked. I appreciate and rejoice in everything that is good.

"Well done, Celine," I say, patting myself on the back.

Life is full of ups and downs—there is no way around it. If you are on a mountaintop, why not enjoy the view instead of thinking of the dark valley that isn't even there at that moment? Although anticipating the worst protected my heart from being hurt, it also deprived me of the simple joys of living.

As I healed, I learned to recognize the voice that told me to expect the worst, and, as if I were standing in front of a mirror, I started talking back.

"Yes, that *may* happen," I would say, "but it's not happening right now."

It was like preaching to my soul, silencing that fearful voice in my head every time. Speaking to myself in this positive, affirming tone is a strength that I continue to develop to this day.

Being the go-getter that I am, once I understood the problem, I wanted it all gone at the snap of a finger—how I wished that I could take a pill that would cure me of it all in a matter of days. But it doesn't work like that. There were no shortcuts on the journey from post-traumatic stress disorder and depression to counseling and recognizing your grief.

Although the year 2015 marked the beginning of my healing journey, I am not yet fully healed. After carrying my heavy burden of trauma for almost twenty-five years, there is still plenty of residue left to clear out —this is going to take time, and it is something I have come to terms with. Through journaling and counseling, having these platforms where I could freely express myself and feel seen and understood, was a great place to start, and something that I still embrace today.

Surrounding myself with a support group in which I can freely breathe out my frustrations, anxiety, hurts, and anything else that bothers me, is crucial if I want to stay on track. Even as we grow stronger and heal from our wounds, life will continue to throw challenges at us and along our paths—at work and at home. When these curveballs catch us in an unstable emotional or psychological state, it is often difficult to respond to them in a healthy way. We might find ourselves with-drawing from clients or colleagues when business is tougher than usual, believing that we are to blame. Often it is external factors outside our control that are responsible for those bad months—busi-ness can become difficult for everyone.

Journaling, writing down my every thought and feeling, changed everything for me—it made me feel truly *alive*, encouraging and empowering me to continue on my healing journey. Reading what I had written down made me feel *seen*, even by *myself*. Writing became a form of release and there was comfort in sharing it. Allowing Gilbert and my close friends to read my thoughts and feelings in their full authenticity liberated me. For the first time, I was showing my face to them with the mask removed, and they were not only able to under-stand my patterns of behavior, but also to hold me accountable.

I noticed how my writing was impacting on others. People would read my notes and draw parallels between my life and their own. Receiving feedback in this manner reinforced my self-esteem, confirming, once again, that my future was worth living for. No matter the size of the impact, I started feeling as if I mattered—that I was making a tangible difference in other people's lives.

God's voice was too loud and too clear to deny that it was coming from anywhere else. He came to me and sat down with me, assigning me a project uniquely designed for me and the people to whom I would be reaching out—my family, my country, and, ultimately, the world. Never in my life did I imagine that I would write and publish a book. Not once did I consider the story my life would tell. I thought that writing books was something done by "other" people. The Devil was there too, as he tried to attack my purpose by poking at my insecurities, filling my thoughts with negativity, and making me believe that nobody would be interested in my story—or that by writing a book, I would be perceived as seeking attention.

It was the overwhelming sense of my God-given purpose that gave me fuel me to break through the mental barriers that were holding me back. I could not see the full picture, but God did. Although He had only revealed a small portion of what He wanted to use me for, it was enough for me to trust Him with the endgame—that it was through Him that I would impact the lives of others through my work in my community, and, most especially, with my generation of Genocide survivors in Rwanda.

What God gives us is the foundation for something far greater than we can begin to imagine—His gifts became the platform that brought healing and spiritual growth to those around me and beyond. I was given the opportunity to make a positive and lasting impact on those who were, and still are, taking similar journeys of their own.

Life does not give us the space to grieve or to gently face our pain. As the daily disappointments and frustrations of life pile on, the pressure builds up to the point that sooner or later, the emotions can no longer be contained and they erupt.

The people I shared my journal entries with were surprised to learn about what I had experienced. They found it difficult to believe that I had lived in this darkness for so long. They found it strange that I had worn my protective mask for so long, externally portraying the complete opposite of what was being manifested inside.

I cannot overstate the importance of reaching out to the people around us who are going through difficult situations in their lives—nobody is ever exempt from life's challenges. If we could all develop antennae to detect people's pain, to hear their unspoken words and their silent screams, to be fully empathetic towards them, instead of simply saying, "*Komera*" (Be strong). Simple questions like, "How are you doing?" go a long way. If someone is grieving the loss of a loved one, give them the space or the platform to express their grief—this is far healthier than allowing them to bottle it up inside in an attempt to appear strong on the outside. People might seem to be energetic and have it all together, but it does not mean that they are not longing to talk to someone. Not everyone who portrays strength is actually strong.

Had someone approached me and asked me how I was *really* doing during the annual commemorations, despite the mask I wore at the time, I have no doubt that, although it would have been extremely uncomfortable, it would have triggered questions inside me. It would have awoken within me a level of self-awareness that may have helped me start my healing journey sooner. I harbor no resentment that no one reached out to me back then, and I would never hold this against anyone because I take full responsibility for my life—we are all on a learning and healing journey.

As the strength of our nation, we are limited when we are mentally and emotionally damaged. There is little that can be done when we are existing rather than living.

Today, I long to play my role in building my country, and not only to reach my full potential but to exceed it. I wonder how much potential would be unleashed and how much we could contribute to our nation and continent if we were all on our healing journeys. It is only when we are in the process of healing that we unlock and discover the hidden treasures that are our gifts and talents. I believe that working together as a healed community will create a society where there are no limitations, where instead of closing doors on people, we open them and give people the space to become the greatest versions of themselves.

36

A Letter To My Ten-Year-Old Self

November 3, 2018

*D**ear little Celine,*

You have been caged and tamed for a long time. Your voice was left unheard for far longer than it should have been. Your pain and loneliness were overlooked and your story was never told. For that, I take full responsibility and I am deeply sorry.

From now on, I promise you that you will never be alone again. Your story has been told and your pain is seen. You have people around the world who, after hearing your story, want to hug and comfort and love you.

You have become the voice of many untold stories. You have the right to be alive, to dream big, to exceed your potential, and be untamed for all of eternity.

As you grow and face challenges out there, remember that your story matters, that you are allowed to not be okay sometimes, but at the same time, it's not okay to stay that way. Seek help, support, and guidance. I guarantee you that this time around, you will be heard and taken care of.

So, fly high, little bird Celine. Fly in the wild and never stop soaring to greater heights because the world is yours and the sky is only the beginning for you.

God is with you until the end of time.

With much love,

Your adult self,

Celine.

37

A Closing Thought

*I*t is Friday morning, the first of February, 2019—National Heroes Day in Rwanda. I am thinking about my nanny, Françoise, who sacrificed her life in the name of love and humanity. I decide to face my giants and do something I have avoided doing for years: I pluck up my courage and look at a photo of two men wearing pink uniforms—the uniform of prisoners. These men were arrested many years earlier. They were among the people who murdered not only my family, but one hundred and fifty other people.

Fifteen years ago, when I first read about their *Gacaca*[1] trial, I resolved to close the door on them—to not get involved in their trial, and to continue with my life as if they did not exist. I also decided to never look at that photo again.

But here it is, lying here in my hands, their faces staring back at me.

Perhaps it is time to dig deeper and reach true forgiveness. Maybe it is time to face my fears and move forward to a whole new level of healing. Wherever this is leading me, perhaps, one day, I will write a book about it—it *is* Heroes Day after all.

. . .

"We must always take sides. Neutrality helps the oppressor, never the victim. Silence encourages the tormentor, never the tormented"

Elie Wiesel (from his book, "Night")

---

1. A Rwandan term which, when loosely translated, means "justice among the grass". They were trials set up and held by local communities to try those accused of participating in the Genocide Against the Tutsi of 1994.

Acknowledgments

To the Nuns' community—"Les petites soeurs de Jesus" of Kicukiro—for opening your doors to hundreds of families, and for creating a home for the orphans. We are blessed beyond measure to have witnessed your selfless sacrifice and love when you took care of us during and after the Genocide. Words will never sufficiently express our gratitude, and there will never be enough thank-yous. You are our angels here on Earth, and we will always hold a special place for you in our hearts.

To my Father, Wilberforce Murengezi—Looking back on your sacrificial life, I am in awe. I always fall short of words when explaining your courage in giving me the best life possible, despite your own wounds after losing most of your family. You found the inner strength to fight for me against all odds, and I will always be grateful to you for that. Daddy, I am your number one fan, and I love you.

To my brother Johnny Murengezi—You have been a warrior all along. Our thirteen-year age gap played a huge role in my sanity after the Genocide. It was as if I had two dads who were prepared to turn the world upside down to protect me and offer me the best life possible, even though you were still hurting inside. To date, I am convinced that no harm will ever reach me as long as my big brother is around. If I am blessed to live long enough, I hope I will be a good aunt to Bryan, Godwin, Shawn, Talia, and a good sister-in-law to Jocelyne (Dudu), just as you have been to me. I wish you true healing, and I love you, bro.

To my husband, Gilbert Kayumba—What can I say? You are one of the reasons that life is worth fighting for. Thank you for always speaking the truth to me. Thank you for not only believing, but *also knowing* that I could do this. I am so thankful that I have you in my life to push me when I am about to give up. Your sense of humor is one of a kind. I look forward to sharing all the good that comes from life with you. I love you always and forever.

To my paternal grandmother, Marion Mukakazana, the anchor and glue of our family—Your dependence on Jesus and unconditional love for people is what stopped my extended family from collapsing after the Genocide. You authentically mourn with those who mourn and rejoice with those who rejoice in a way that inspires everyone who knows you. I like to believe that I am your favorite grandchild as an excuse to always be pampered by your affection. You are my hero and the vision of who I am becoming—you are who I want to become when I grow up. I love you to the moon and back.

To my Aunt Helene Sebuharara (Maman Lily) and my Aunt Dorothe Mugeni—You are each a true representation of ferocity and gentleness residing in one person. You are my mother's legacy, and your love and affection for me have kept me going until today. Your home is my home, and your doors are always open for anything that I might need in this life. Thank you for modeling true, noble values that are a precious legacy to my cousins and me. I love you very much.

To my friends that became family, especially Josiane Musasirwa, Denise Umunyana, Dora Umutoni, Melissa Muyenzi, and Yasmine Umutoni—my heroines and wonder women of all time. You deserve a Nobel Prize for keeping up with my personality disorders and staying around for better or for worse. Sincerely, I admire you. I look forward to continuing doing life with you, especially now that I have so much to offer from within. The future is smiling at us with great rewards—watch this space. I love you big time.

To my *"lunch latte"* friends, Alain Sabineza and Laure Iyaga—You are my partners in art. I never imagined that a counseling class would award me with accountability partners that would become such an incredible support system throughout my healing journey. This memoir exists because of you and I look forward to seeing our many future projects unfold and flourish. I love you both very much.

To each of my family members, to my friends in Rwanda and around the world, and to everyone who contributed to my life in one way or another, thank you for being part of my healing journey. I will forever be grateful.

To my book editors, Phyllis Lerner, Gael Tunga Rutembesa, and Phillipa Mitchell—the enablers of this memoir. It was not an easy task to convert the notes from my therapy sessions, the hand-written letters, and my voice notes into a format that people could read. Thank you for your support and for your professional work.

Above all, I would like to thank God. While putting this memoir together, I had many doubts, hesitations, and insecurities. You strengthened and validated me in a way that nobody else could. You raised an army of passionate people to support me throughout the process. I could never have done this without your everlasting love, guidance, and inspiration. I look forward to driving through the next chapters of my life with You at the wheel.

Gallery 2

Celine's brother Johnny (*left*), with her father Murengezi Wilberforce (*right*)

Celine with her husband Gilbert, at a restaurant, gorilla-tracking adventure and in Mombasa, Kenya.

Grandmother Marion, at Celine's traditional wedding day.

Celine with her two Aunties, Helene Sebuharara (Maman Lily) and Dorothe Mugeni (right).

Celine with her sister Lyrette and her brother Michael in Kigali, 2017.

Gilbert and Celine on their civil wedding day, with their friends, Josiane Musasirwa (*left*), Denise Umunyana and Yasmine Umutoni (*right*).

Celine with her friend Melissa Muyenzi.

Gilbert and Celine with their friend, Dora Mutoni.

Celine's partners' in Art, Laure Iyaga (*left*), Alain Sabineza (*center*)

Celine with her business partner Denise, at the Africa Youth Connect Summit in Kigali, 2018.

Celine with Sister Leoncie from "Les petites soeurs de Jesus de Kicukiro".

Printed in Great Britain
by Amazon

77171634R00097